BEING THE BELIEVING

Living Out the Beatitudes

Thomas McCracken

D0967280

Sermon To Book
www.sermontobook.com

Being The Believing / Thomas McCracken
ISBN-13: 9780692378830
ISBN-10: 0692378839

I want to thank my Lord for His love and patience that have shown me, as His child, that Being the Believing is not about perfect people, but imperfect, dysfunctional, scarred and hurting people letting out what He has let in.

Furthermore, this book is dedicated to all of the genuine believers who have lived before God with a heart of integrity and have impacted my life greatly. Standing tall among these "giants of the faith" is my wife of 24 years. While others had told me of Christianity, she was the first to show me real faith lived out. Laurie McCracken was the first in my life who demonstrated what Being the Believing really was, and because of that, I received Christ and discovered for myself the joy in living a victorious Christian life through the beatitudes.

In addition to my wife, I dedicate this book to the most supportive, loving and mature congregation of believers, CommUNITY Church (www.communitychurchva.com). Without their patience and support, the research and time to make this book a reality would never have happened.

CONTENTS

"Following Christ is more than a Sunday morning event. *Being the Believing* reminds followers of Jesus Christ that we are to *be* the church, not just go to church. We must not only nod our heads and say 'amen,' but we are also to be what we believe. ... [Becoming] the salt of the earth and light of the world ... begins with *Being the Believing*." — **Dr. Brian Autry, Executive Director, SBC of Virginia**

"I am so grateful for this important book, written by my friend Tom McCracken. He has pointed to the beauty of the Beatitudes by focusing on the Beautiful One: Jesus. As Tom writes, 'God has given us all that we need, not to do good, but to be good, which is what *Being the Believing* is all about.'" — **Dr. Don Cockes, Missionary**

Jonathan Falwell

Foreword

One of the primary callings of any pastor is to lead the people whom he has the privilege of pastoring into a deeper relationship with Christ. It is not enough that a pastor simply informs them of the message of the Gospel, while certainly this is key. Pastors have a strong desire, and a God-given command, to help people grow in their faith.

In Mark 16, Matthew 28 and Acts 1, Jesus gave us our marching orders in no uncertain terms. He said, "Go into all the world and preach the Gospel..." He told us to "...make disciples of all the nations..." and to go into "...Jerusalem, Judea, Samaria and the ends of the earth." Those are not suggestions, they are commands. While it is clear that Gospel proclamation is vital, it is also clear that making disciples is also vital.

This is why I am so excited about this book, *Being the Believing*, by Pastor Tom McCracken. His passion and desire to help people become all that God intended is clear. And, there is no greater place in all the world to learn how to live out our faith than from the teachings of Christ, and more specifically, the Beatitudes. Tom has spent a great deal of time praying over each of the eight blessings and encouragements given by Christ to mankind and, as a result, shares his heart in these pages.

Jesus wants each of us to understand how important it is to live out our faith on a daily basis. He wants us to embrace the Great Commission, but also the Great Commandment. Jesus, when asked about the greatest commandment, said it is to, "…love the Lord your God with all of your heart…and the second is like it, to love your neighbor as yourself." That's why this book is so important and so timely.

This book will help you recognize why we must seek God's Word and way in our lives and embrace His way of living. In doing so, we will strengthen our daily walk and prepare for any situation that might come our way. As Pastor Tom so eloquently writes, it's not nearly enough that we do good, we must be good. And there is no possibility of truly "being good" unless we are fully immersed in the deeper, Christian life that Christ intends.

As you read this book, determine to not only read the words on the page but rather let them truly sink into your heart. Allow the meaning behind each of the beatitudes to take hold in your mind. Make the commitment that this won't be just another book for you to read, let it be the catalyst for you to apply God's desire and plan in your life. This is what Jesus intended when He gave those eight great encouragements.

In Acts 1:8, we are told by Christ, "But you shall receive power when the Holy Spirit has come upon you;

and you shall be witnesses to Me in Jerusalem, and in all Judea and Samaria, and to the end of the earth." In this verse, we find a promise and a demand. First, Jesus promises that we *shall* receive power. And then, we are commanded that we *shall* be witnesses. *Being The Believing* will teach us all how to use that power and fulfill that command to change the world.

Read this book and allow it to change your life!

— *Jonathan Falwell*

Introduction

*Seeing the crowds, he went up on the mountain, and when he sat down, his disciples came to him. — **Matthew 5:1***

There is a big difference between *doing good* and *being good*. And the fact that many do not know the difference is the reason why there are Christians feeling unloved living in a world that remains unchanged.

I wasted many years of my life trying to *do good* to please those around me: my parents, family, counselors, teachers, bosses and friends, all of these folks coming at me from different directions and perspectives with well-intentioned voices echoing the same sentiment, "Tom, *do* good!" And, for many years, I felt like a failure for not living up to that expectation. I never dreamed that one day I could *be* good.

Again, there is a big difference between *doing good* and *being good*. That difference is found in the beatitudes.

You are wasting your time if you are trying to do good without being good first. That is the beauty of the beatitudes: that God has given us all that we need, not to *do good*, but to *be good,* which is what Being the Believing is all about.

I am so excited that you have decided to make the investment and take the time to join me in this journey through the beatitudes. I will be praying that, after reading this book, you would have the confidence and assurance that come from an intimate relationship with God, through Jesus. And that you would have a desire to take all that He has given you and get on mission for Him; that you would be able to say, "I am Being the Believing!"

CHAPTER ONE

From Rags to Riches

Seeing the crowds, he went up on the mountain, and when he sat down, his disciples came to him. And he opened his mouth and taught them, saying: Blessed are the poor in spirit, for theirs is the kingdom of heaven.
— Matthew 5:1-3

The first word of Matthew 5:1, "seeing," has captivated me theologically and personally, as does Hebrews 1:1, which says, "Long ago, at many times and in many ways, God *spoke* to our fathers by the prophets."

What an amazing event! God did not have to speak; He was not lonely; He did not need a new friend; He was not incomplete without us; and we certainly did not deserve the voice of Almighty God. Yet He chose to speak anyway.

And here, we find that God sees us. Let me jump ahead in Matthew 5:1 to the words, "he went up on the mountain, and when he sat down…"

In order to understand the significance of Jesus "seeing" the crowds, we must delve into the theology behind this statement.

In this simple, yet profound, statement, the Apostle Matthew is making some Old Testament Moses comparisons to the New Testament Christ. He is saying that just as Moses, the deliverer of the nation of Israel, went up to a mountain (Exodus 19:3) and sat down (Deuteronomy 9:9), so Jesus Christ, the better Deliverer, went up to a mountain and sat down (Matthew 5:1). As Moses gave a law that would be binding, Jesus gave liberty that would be freeing.

By comparing Moses to Christ, Matthew seeks to prove that the words of Jesus carry divine authority, since He is the better Moses.

One of my favorite quotes from C. S. Lewis is, "Either Jesus was Liar, Lunatic or Lord." To believe that Jesus Christ was more than a prophet, miracle worker, teacher, healer or priest is to believe that He is the risen and living Savior, seated before the disciples and crowds, speaking to humanity through the Sermon on the Mount. By comparing Moses to Christ, Matthew seeks to prove that the words of Jesus carry divine authority, since He is the better Moses.

Now, having established that Jesus is the Old Testament-prophesied Messiah, we can look at this word "seeing." As I stated earlier, this word has captivated me theologically and personally. To know that God, with all He has going on in the universe, sees *us* is compelling to say the least.

Even more profound is the understanding that the Greek word for "see" implies a deep knowledge of the unseen. In other words, only God has the unique, supernatural ability to see the real you—the you that is never shared with anyone else: the late night struggles, the deep-rooted pain, the past hurts, the emotional scars, your hopes and dreams, your fears and worries. God sees *that* you!

There are 196 countries on this planet, with as many as 27,000 people groups representing over 7 billion people, yet God sees you.

There are 196 countries on this planet, with as many as 27,000 people groups representing over 7 billion people, yet God sees **you**. And with God, to see you is to *know* you. In fact, God knows you better than anyone, yet chooses to love you more than everyone! The theological implications captivate me, and the personal ramifications encourage me.

When Moses went up to the mountain of God and approached the burning bush, he had a heavy heart. His people were slaves under the sadistic hands of the Egyptian taskmasters and ruled by the godless Pharaoh.

Moses himself had spent 40 years on the backside of the wilderness, struggling through guilt, shame, regret, fear, and purpose. I am sure he felt that nobody cared, that he was all alone and that God did not see what was going on. Then the Lord said, "I have surely *seen* the affliction of my people who are in Egypt and have heard their cry because of their taskmasters. I *know* their sufferings" (Exodus 3:7). For God to see you is for God to know you, and for God to know you is for God to care about you.

When we really understand that God sees us, knows us, cares about us, and is able to help us, our natural response is to position ourselves as close to Him as possible.

Some people see but don't care; others care but don't see; and still others don't see or care. It's life changing to know that God both sees and cares. No wonder verse 1 ends with "…his disciples came to him."

When we really understand that God sees us, knows us, cares about us, and is able to help us, our natural response is to position ourselves as close to Him as possible. That's why, since my salvation 24 years ago, I can't get enough of my God: any time His Word is being taught and preached and His people are meeting, fellowshipping, praying and serving, I am right in the middle of the action! I want to be as close to Him as I can get.

Please believe that the God of the universe sees, cares and is able. And because He cares, He has earned the right to our attention. "And he opened his mouth and taught them" (Matthew 5:2).

According to Matthew 4:16, these people had been sitting in isolated darkness. They were lonely, overwhelmed and defeated until Jesus called them with the most powerful two words one can ever be obedient to: "Follow me." They had been drawn to the light, rescued from their depravity, and compelled to listen to the voice of God because of the invitation to His love.

Boy, does that sound like us. There was a time that we were in darkness, controlled by our emotions and feelings, yielding to sin, isolated, overwhelmed and defeated. And rightfully so, for we were children of wrath destined to spend an eternity in hell, separated from the love of God forever (Romans 6:23). But then God "gave his only Son, that whoever believes in him should not perish but have eternal life" (John 3:16).

Jesus has rescued us from our depravity, saved us by His sacrifice, redeemed us through His grace, showered us with His blessings, and compelled us to listen to His voice because of His love. He has brought us from rags to riches, and I would say that He has earned the right to our attention!

In Deuteronomy 18:15, Moses writes, "The Lord your God will raise up for you a prophet like me from among you, from your brothers—it is to him you shall *listen*."

In Matthew 5:3, He's saying that:

God's blessings only come to those who seek His approval!

Now let me draw your attention to the word "blessed" and point out what it does not mean:

- Blessed does not mean happiness that is tethered to feelings and emotions, which are anchored to externals. This word is not referring to those moments of emotion when you receive a bonus in your paycheck or a compliment from a friend.

The word "blessed" *is* speaking of an inner, complete satisfaction that is tethered to salvation in Christ, not subject to emotion, fear or circumstance. An inner joy that is established in God, not given by this world, so it can't be taken by this world. "Blessed" can simply mean *approved by God.*

So, we could read verse 3 thusly: "Approved by God are the poor in spirit, for theirs is the kingdom of heaven."

After the Apostle Matthew gets our attention on the One worthy of our attention, we find the very first thing Jesus says to these new disciples, after he called them to follow Him in Matthew 4:19, is "Blessed are the poor in spirit."

"Poor in spirit" presents some more interesting Greek words, but again, let me start by pointing out what they do not mean:

- Poor in spirit does not mean that you have no value: God does not bless someone because they have no value, as all of humanity has value in His eyes. "The Lord your God is in your midst, a mighty one who will save; he will rejoice over you with gladness; he will quiet you by his love; he will exult over you with loud singing" (Zephaniah 3:17).

Don't you dare believe the devil's lie that you have no value; you are a creation of the living God, and He loves you with an everlasting love. The Bible says that you were created in His image and in His likeness (Genesis 1:27) and that you were formed and fashioned while you were in your mother's womb (Psalm 139:13). Furthermore, there is nothing you can do to cause God to love you any more than He already does. And there is nothing you can do to cause God to love you any less; He is in love with you! So, "blessed" does not mean that God only approves people who have no value since everyone has value, as we are all created by our God.

- And, being poor in spirit does not mean that you have no money! For the Apostle Peter declared, "Truly I understand that God shows no partiality" (Acts 10:34). God does not approve those who live with a dirt floor and a cardboard roof any more than He does the owner of a mansion in Beverly Hills. He loves every one of us the same as He died for all of us the same. So, "blessed" is not speaking of a lack of materialism.

- And, the word "blessed" does not speak of a showy humility; it is not speaking of someone who takes great pride in their humility! Martyn Lloyd-Jones tells of meeting such a man on one of his preaching missions. When Dr. Lloyd-Jones arrived at a train station, a man asked for the minister's suitcase and, in fact, almost ripped it from his hand, saying, "I am a deacon in the church where you are preaching tomorrow. You know, I am a mere nobody, a very unimportant man. Really. I do not count; I am not a great man in the church; I am just one of those men who carry the bag for the minister." Lloyd-Jones observes, "He was anxious that I should know what a humble man he was, how 'poor in spirit.' Yet by his anxiety to make it known, he was denying the very thing he was trying to establish." So, "blessed" does not speak of someone who takes great pride in their humility!

So, if this word "poor" is not connected to value, money or showy humility, what does it mean? The Greek word for "poor" employed here actually means to "cower and cringe like a beggar, and to be pitiful, inferior and worthless." If only we had a scriptural example of this word being fleshed out by a life. Oh, we do! In Luke 16:19, it says, "There was a rich man who was clothed in purple and fine linen and who feasted sumptuously every day. And at his gate was laid a *poor* man named Lazarus, covered with sores, who desired to be fed with what fell from the rich man's table. Moreover, even the dogs came and licked his sores" (Luke 16:19–21).

Paul was spot-on when he declared, "I am the chief of all sinners" (1 Timothy 1:15).

This poor man had no control of his life. He was so bankrupt that he was completely dependent upon the help of others to survive. He was so desperately poor that the only way he could even receive a crumb off a table for sustenance was to acknowledge his beggarly poor state and to receive the help that was offered. When we teach, read or even preach through this account in Luke, we often focus on our role in helping this poor man. In fact, I preached a message a couple years ago titled, "Who Has God Laid at Your Gate?" which outlined our need to love and care for those around us by being gospel-driven. However, there is another way to view this text. And, it is tied to Matthew 5:3 through the word "poor."

As much as it may hurt your self-image, the word "poor" in Luke 16, which is used to describe a sore-ridden, disease-carrying, poorer-than-poor reproach to society, is the same word used in Matthew 5:3. So, let's try reading this text again. Matthew 5:3 could say, "Approved of God are those who cower and cringe like a beggar: the pitiful, inferior and worthless, theirs is the kingdom of heaven." The hymn "Rock of Ages" nails this text with words like these: "Nothing in my hand I bring, simply to the cross I cling."

Peter had it right when he declared, "Go away from me, Lord; I am a sinful man" (Luke 5:8).

Paul was spot-on when he declared, "I am the chief of all sinners" (1 Timothy 1:15).

> *You must come to the place where you believe, really and truly believe, that you are a wretched, miserable, beggarly poor, sinning worm that needs someone, outside of and bigger than you, to help and rescue you.*

Isaiah knew this truth when he cried, "Woe is me! For I am lost; for I am a man of unclean lips" (Isaiah 6:5).

The mighty Gideon, who delivered Israel with just 300 men, acknowledged to God, "I am the least in my father's house."

The Isaac Watts hymn written in 1885, "At the Cross," used to have it right when the stanza was sung, "Would He devote that sacred head, for such a *worm* as I."

Newer hymnals have replaced the words "for such a *worm* as I" with "for such a *sinner* as I" or even worse, "for such a *one* as I." In our current American church culture where self-esteem prevails, we don't like anything that may damage our beautiful image.

> *My prayer is that you will be able to declare, through a heart of integrity, the words of William Carey, "A wretched, poor, and helpless worm, on Thy kind arms I fall."*

King David, a man after God's own heart, would not have sung "for such a one as I," for he had no problem acknowledging his worm-like status when he declared in Psalm 22:6, "I am a worm and not a man…"

The great William Carey, a Baptist missionary in the 1700s and 1800s, known as the Father of Modern Missions, had no issue with this word either, for on his gravestone are the words, "A wretched, poor, and helpless worm, on Thy kind arms I fall."

You must come to the place where you believe, really and truly believe, that you are a wretched, miserable, beggarly poor, sinning worm that needs someone, outside of and bigger than you, to help and rescue you.

We must embrace the formula found in Isaiah 41:13–14, "For I am the Lord your God, who upholds your right hand, who says to you, 'do not fear, I will help you.' Do not fear, you *worm* Jacob, you men of Israel; I will help you,' declares the Lord, 'And your Redeemer is the Holy One of Israel."

For all of the worms out there, like me, you must understand that God's eternal blessings only come to those who seek His approval! Are you ready to be blessed by God today?

My prayer is that you will be able to declare, through a heart of integrity, the words of William Carey, "A wretched, poor, and helpless worm, on Thy kind arms I fall."

> *Blessed are the poor in spirit, for theirs is the kingdom of heaven.*
> — *Matthew 5:3*

CHAPTER TWO

Good Grief

Blessed are they that mourn: for they shall be comforted.
— *Matthew 5:4*

The eight beatitudes should be viewed as stepping stones that are all building on each other, ultimately culminating in a powerful position and blessed state. In the business world, we call this the corporate ladder: you start in an entry-level position, work and claw your way up, and by the time you reach that last rung, you are rewarded with that corner office, a giant pay raise, position, popularity, promotion and power.

I like to view the beatitudes as our Lord's version of the corporate ladder, a "beatitudinal ladder" if you will. As we start at entry level, we work our way up through faith and maturity so that by the time we reach the top, we are well equipped to enjoy the reward found on that last rung.

The first rung of this ladder was found in Matthew 5:3, where Jesus stated: "Blessed are the poor in spirit, for theirs is the kingdom of heaven." Remember, this word "blessed" does not mean happy; happiness is subjective. Blessed speaks of an inner satisfaction tethered to salvation in Christ, not subject to emotions, feelings and fear, nor dependent upon circumstances.

So, when God blesses us, He is actually approving us. This is a lesson that we all need to hear: to stop seeking approval from creation and to align ourselves solely to the approval of the Creator. How freeing it is when you stop trying to please everyone around you and simply live for the One within you!

If you are seeking the approval of God, the first step is to acknowledge that you are poor in spirit, or spiritually bankrupt.

You can go around exhausting yourself, trying to please everyone who comes into your life. Peace only comes when we endeavor to find rest in simply seeking the approval of God.

So, if you are seeking the approval of God, the first step is to acknowledge that you are poor in spirit, or spiritually bankrupt. Admit that salvation is not based on what you do, or who you are, but on what He has done and who He is!

Salvation is a very personal matter between you and the Lord. It's when you come to a place in your life where you recognize your beggarly poor state, your need for rescue, and run to the cross to find there is still room for you! That is the first rung on this ladder. It must start here.

Our next beatitude found in Matthew 5:4 says, "Blessed are those who mourn, for they shall be comforted."

To recognize our sin is to mourn over our condition.

To recognize our sin is to mourn over our condition. The reason that so many churches have lost their power is because so many Christians have lost their focus. And when you take your eyes off of Christ, they fall on people. Many "Christians" are causing so many problems because they are so focused on everyone else. Some of the most bitter, critical, cynical, unforgiving people you will ever meet sit next to you in church, Sunday after Sunday. That is the result of taking your eyes off of Christ.

This is the main reason 4,000 churches close their doors every single year in our country. Churches are full of people who are so inwardly focused they have no outwardly concern. Vance Havner highlighted this phenomenon when he declared, "The world has become so churchy and the church so worldly, that you can't tell the two apart." Church members might have walked down an aisle, said a prayer, been baptized and now sing from the choir loft about the power in the blood, but there is no power in their lives because they have never been transformed and regenerated through the gospel of Jesus Christ. In fact, the only evidence many folks offer to be classified as "Christian" are the fish magnets on their cars, Christian music playing through their radios, "Property of God" t-shirts on their backs, and their names on a church membership roll. There is no change, no difference.

How do we fix this? By mourning over our sin. By regaining the internal focus required by our Lord. Jesus was an expert at redirecting focus. Remember the woman who was caught in adultery? She had a crowd of men lined up and ready to stone her because that crowd had lost its focus; they had set their sights on someone else and overlooked their own sin. Jesus reminded them of the sin in their lives, thereby getting them focused internally once again. That is where we all need to be: internally focused, mourning over our own sin.

To recognize our sin is to mourn over our condition. I was watching a Mark Lowry video the other day, and he stood before a full house and talked about how Jesus started the church with the outcasts of society—the prostitutes, drunkards, fornicators, adulterers, tax collectors, smelly fishermen, and even a Samaritan woman. And the church grew! It grew because one beggar would tell another beggar where the food was. Now that the church has grown, we are inside holding the doors closed, not letting anyone else in, because we are judging those outside—because they sin differently than we do. It is time we fling those doors open and let them in so that they can experience the peace, position, and power we have found through the gospel of Jesus Christ!

> *The key to our text: recognizing your own sin and mourning over your own condition.*

Mark then stated that he has hated the sin and loved the sinner too long. He said, "I don't have time to hate your sin. Hate your own sin! How about you hate your sin and I'll hate my sin and then we just love on each other?" And, there it is, the key to our text: recognizing your own sin and mourning over your own condition.

You might say, "But I don't have sin in my life." I guarantee you do.

"As it is written: 'None is righteous, no, not one; no one understands; no one seeks for God. All have turned aside; together they have become worthless; no one does good, not even one'" (Romans 3:10–12).

Did you notice that statement, "no one seeks for God"? You did not find God, for He was never lost! You are the sinner. You are the one who is lost, and it is God who must find you. And the only way He can find you bobbing around life's ocean of trials, in the darkness of your sin, is for you to send up the Matthew 5:3 beacon, confessing you are spiritually bankrupt in need of rescue. You must believe in your heart and confess with your mouth that Jesus Christ died and rose again, and willfully and purposefully surrender to His will for your life by repenting of your sins and following Him.

Once we are redeemed and rescued, we can't help but love our Father. It has been said that people only know as much about us as we let them know about us. Here is the wonderful truth: God knows everything about us—where we have been, what we have done, what we think, and even what we have yet to do—and He still loves us! Knowing about that kind of love, we now have a desire to please Him, so we mourn over our sin.

As with you, there was a time I did not mourn over my sin but celebrated it. During my high school years, we lived in an Airstream trailer next to an orange grove; you can't get more country than that! So, if I were to describe my life before Christ in country lingo, I would say something like this: I was a drinkin', smokin', cussin', fussin', hatin' heathen who was lookin' for love in all the wrong places, hopeless, lost, defeated and broken in need of a fixin'…but then I heard an old, old story:

"How a Savior came from glory, how He gave His life on Calvary to save a wretch like me; I heard about His groaning, of His precious blood's atoning, then I repented of my sins and won the victory.

"O victory in Jesus, my Savior, forever. He sought me and bought me with His redeeming blood; He loved me ere I knew Him and all my love is due Him, He plunged me to victory, beneath the cleansing flood." [1]

I know what it took to reconcile this sinner to a holy, almighty God. It took Jesus to don the robes of humanity, living for 33 years, going through a mock trial, suffering, bleeding and ending His life by hanging on a cruel Roman cross suspended between His home and His creation, being rejected by both. It took God's everything, His Only Begotten Son. So, knowing what it took to forgive me and to set me free, understanding that He knows me better than anyone yet chooses to love me more than everyone, I completely surrender my life to His love. That is why, when I look at my sin, I mourn, for I am now aware that it hurts the very heart of the only One who has loved me with an everlasting love.

And, in addition to being concerned enough about our own sin that we actually mourn over it, we mourn over the sins of others since we are now aware that their sin hurts the heart of our Father God as well.

> *My eyes shed streams of tears, because people do not keep your law.*
> — **Psalm 119:136**

The words David chose to use speak of utter distress and weakness. In other words, the psalmist is saying that he is crippled and in deep grieving. Not the kind of crying one does when a toe is stubbed, but the kind of mourning that occurs in the loss of a child. Why is David that upset? Because when someone you love is hurt, you hurt, and our Father hurts when His creation sins. We hear plenty about how sin brings the judgment of God, that God hates sin and punishes the wicked evildoer. But there is another element found in Ephesians 4:29–30: "Let no corrupt communication proceed out of your mouth, but that which is good to the use of edifying, that it may minister grace unto the hearers. And *grieve* not the Holy Spirit of God, whereby ye are sealed unto the day of redemption."

> *We should mourn over the sins of others because we are motivated by the supernatural love of God to actually care for others. Jeremiah looked at the sins of humanity and wept so much that he was known as the weeping prophet.*

Firstly, this text reveals that what grieves the heart of God within the church of God is the disruption of unity caused by the sin of gossip, slander and contention.

But don't miss what these sins do: they grieve the Holy Spirit of God. This word means, "to afflict with sorrow, to cause pain and anguish, to trouble and to torture." Keeping this in context, according to Ephesians 4:29–30, people who speak against each other or against God are torturing God.

> *Not only was Paul willing to postpone heaven, but he was also ready to replace someone in hell. Paul, Jeremiah and Jesus looked at the sins of humanity and cared.*

Let me simply ask, in light of what Jesus went through—being rejected, beaten, whipped, forced to carry a cross and nailed to that same cross on a hill called Mount Calvary, where He suffered, bled and died—has He not been tortured enough? Should we live in such a way as to torture and crucify our Lord again and again? God forbid. So, it should hurt us when Christians sin because we should not want our Lord to suffer anymore.

And we should mourn over the sins of others because we are motivated by the supernatural love of God to actually care for others. Jeremiah looked at the sins of humanity and wept so much that he was known as the weeping prophet.

Likewise, Jesus Christ was thought by some to be Jeremiah because when He looked at the sins of humanity, He wept. The Apostle Paul revealed his care for others when he stated in Philippians 1:23: "I am in a straight betwixt two, having a desire to depart and be with Christ which is far better; nevertheless to remain here is more needful for you."

The Apostle Paul was willing to postpone heaven for others. Yet even more care for others was evident when he stated in Romans 9, "For I could wish that I myself were cursed and cut off from Christ for the sake of my brothers, those of my own race, the people of Israel."

Don't miss that. Not only was Paul willing to postpone heaven, but he was also ready to replace someone in hell. Paul, Jeremiah and Jesus looked at the sins of humanity and cared.

When was the last time you really looked at the sins of humanity through the lens of Matthew 5:4 and wept because you cared?

The church has become quite proficient in letting this world know what they are against but tragically leaving them wondering who they are for.

To see others in sin is to know the separation they face. The reason that so many churches have lost their power is because so many Christians have lost their focus. And what is our focus? Matthew 28:16–20, the Great Commission, to go out into this world and make disciples! To care enough about the sins of others that we actually leave the doors of the church building, enter the mission field, and boldly proclaim that Jesus Christ has been resurrected and that our Lord lives!

Too many in the church today have lost focus and are content with where the church is. They have the attitude: "I'm saved; my wife is saved; our children are saved; and we just don't give a rip about anyone else!"

The church has become quite proficient in letting this world know what they are against but tragically leaving them wondering who they are for.

In a recent *Southern Baptist Convention Life* magazine article, it was revealed that the number of folks who are making decisions for Christ and following that decision with believer's baptism has not been this low since 1948. Frank Page reminded Southern Baptists of a time when the Convention set a goal of eight-to-one (8:1); for every eight Southern Baptists, we should see one convert every year, an 8:1 ratio. Now? The ratio of church members to baptisms is more than fifty-to-one (51:1). This tragically sounds like a joke: how many Baptists does it take to share the gospel and win one for the kingdom each year? Apparently 51.

Too many in the church today have lost focus and are content with where the church is. Speaking to this, Dr. Brian Autry, who serves as Executive Director of the Southern Baptist Conservatives of Virginia, a partnership of 640 Southern Baptist churches, recently proclaimed at a gathering of pastors in Roanoke, "Many have the attitude: 'I'm saved; my wife is saved; our children are saved; and we just don't give a rip about anyone else!'"

When was the last time you presented the gospel to a lost man, woman, boy or girl? If I were to ask your classmates, coworkers, neighbors and friends about the last time you told them the story of that Old Rugged Cross, how would they respond?

All your friends saved? Yes? Then get new friends!

I am glad you're saved and your household is all set; I really am. I am excited that you can proclaim that all of your friends and family are saved and that your circle of influence is all accounted for on the train to glory!

If that's the case, it's time to move on to another harvest. All your friends saved? Yes? Then get new friends! I am thankful that you have experienced the power and grace of God, that He was able to save you to the uttermost; and if you're any kind of sinner like me, you know that we took a whole lot of saving! But it's time to get busy!

We are surrounded by a world full of lost people, many of whom do not even see themselves as lost. Yet even more tragic is that with all of these folks facing eternal damnation, we do not have enough transformed believers making much of Jesus by bringing these unbelievers the good news.

We have the light, the hope, the power, the peace, the way, the truth and the life inside us, yet in spite of folks all around us with a desperate need to hear eternal good news, we are refusing to "give an account of that hope that is within us" (1 Peter 3:15).

Oh, we are singing in the choir, teaching Sunday school and preaching sermons. We are in church every time the doors are open and claim our lives are being changed, yet the harvest is still full of people on their way to eternal separation because we simply do not have laborers for the field.

We have played around long enough. It's time for us to go out, look around, reach down, open up and let the gospel go forth.

Mourning over our sin and the sins of others always translates to caring for others. Do we really care about the clerk, the waitress, the mechanic, our nurse or doctor, our exterminator, our neighbors, our classmates and our coworkers?

We have played around long enough. It's time for us to go out, look around, reach down, open up and let the gospel go forth.

Bringing ourselves to a place where we mourn over our sin and the sins of those around us makes us very uncomfortable, yet only through mourning can we hope to receive comfort. "Blessed are those who mourn, for they shall be comforted" (Matthew 5:4).

Chuck Colson, in his book *Who Speaks for God?* writes, "In sin we carry around baggage, scars, fear, guilt, shame and doubt. Yet Jesus Christ tells us all today that when we mourn over that very sin, He will give comfort. He is telling you today to look to yourself, acknowledge your sin, mourn over it, and immediately you will see your baggage dropped, scars healed, fear replaced with trust, shame changed to boldness and doubt converted to faith." [2]

Aren't you tired? Isn't life hard enough without the internal struggles? Don't you long for a safe place to fall, a time when you are so overwhelmed with acceptance, power, joy and love that you just want to leave your tears in the valley and dance on the mountaintop?

Mourn over your sin. This is the paradox of the beatitudes, "truth flipped on its head." If you want comfort, you must mourn. If you want to be blessed by God, you must weep over your sins and the sins of those around you, knowing that as you cry out, you will receive the comfort only God can give as the Great Physician.

May there be showers of blessings for His church today!

You see, grief can be good.

Blessed are they that mourn: for they shall be comforted.
— *Matthew 5:4*

CHAPTER THREE

Gentle Giants

Blessed are the meek: for they shall inherit the earth.
— ***Matthew 5:5***

There are eight beatitudes found in Matthew 5. They define and describe the responsibilities and expectations of the Christian and reveal the rewards for such a life.

Scholars have divided the eight beatitudes into two areas: the first four deal with our relationship with God, and the last four our relationship with each other.

If we have learned anything from the law, Judaism, it is that we lack the capacity to fulfill it and are void of the desire to complete it. This is the beauty of Christianity: all that God requires of us He provides us with both the capacity to fulfill and the desire to complete.

Culture after culture has tried legislating morality. In other words, blanket external resources over humanity, and hope they do well.

This has always failed, and it always will. Why? We simply lack the capacity and desire to do good. "As it is written: 'None is righteous, no, not one; no one understands; no one seeks for God. All have turned aside; together they have become worthless; no one does good, not even one" (Romans 3:10–12).

Before God lays out His expectations of living for Him, He reveals the capacity and desire that come from Him.

The beauty of the beatitudes is found in the division: The first four are our relationship with God, and the last four our relationship with each other.

In other words, before God lays out His expectations of living for Him, He reveals the capacity and desire that come from Him.

Secondly, in this division of the beatitudes we find something else amazing that Christ has done. From the initial Ten Commandments in Judaism, there sprung over 600 commandments recognized today.

Don't miss what Jesus Christ has done and the freeing beauty found in the religion of Christianity. During the earthly ministry of Jesus Christ, someone stepped up and asked Him, "Teacher, which is the greatest commandment in the Law?" And he said to him, "You shall love the Lord your God with all your heart and with all your soul and with all your mind. This is the great and first commandment. And a second is like it: You shall love your neighbor as yourself. On these two commandments depend all the Law and the Prophets" (Matthew 22:36–40).

To start a relationship with God, you must come to the place in your life where you need a relationship with God.

Did you get that? Jesus looked at Judaism, with its hundreds of complicated laws, and basically said, "Love God and love each other, and I will give you the capacity and desire to do it!"

So, our first rung on the beatitudinal ladder, our first step in our relationship to God, was found in Matthew 5:3, "Blessed are the poor in spirit, for theirs is the kingdom of heaven." To start a relationship with God, you must come to the place in your life where you *need* a relationship with God.

The second step in our relationship with God is found in Matthew 5:4, which says, "Blessed are those who mourn, for they shall be comforted."

Once we discover that God loves us and we surrender to that love by loving Him, we hurt when He hurts. And what hurts Him the most is when His creation sins against Him.

So, we mourn over our sins and the sins of others because those sins hurt the very heart of the only One who has loved us with an everlasting love.

Now we come to the third of four steps in our relationship with God, found in Matthew 5:5, which says, "Blessed are the meek, for they shall inherit the earth."

Let me define meekness by first stating what it is not. Meekness is not:

A Lack of Confidence, or Being Wishy-Washy

Meekness is not describing someone who is shy, withdrawn, or introverted, or someone who goes with the flow of culture. Paul tells us that, "God gave us a spirit not of fear but of power and love and self-control" (1 Timothy 1:7). If anyone ought to be walking around with confidence and boldness, exhibiting power in their lives and demonstrating conviction, it should be a child of the King!

So, weakness does not speak of someone who is void of confidence or without convictions. Neither does it speak of:

Weakness

And meekness is not speaking of someone who is a doormat to those around them. There are two reasons Christians allow others to dominate, control, manipulate or use them: In the first group we find those who are motivated extrinsically. These folks have been told for so long by so many that they are worthless, no good and inferior, that they now believe within themselves that they have no voice and no value.

The second group is motivated intrinsically. These folks have a desire to be pushed around by others because they think meekness means weakness and that by being weak for God, they stand to be rewarded. These folks represent a kind of self-sadistic Christian martyr, in that they believe, by their sacrificial display of weakness, they stand to be rewarded by God through blessings.

Paul says in Philippians 4:13, "I can do all things through him who strengthens me." Christ does not expect weakness, for it is He Himself who provides strength.

So, if meekness does not mean weakness, what does it mean? The Greek word for "meek" in our text is a picture-word that was used for at least three things: *a gentle breeze, a soothing medicine, and a tamed wild animal.*

A gentle breeze: An unstoppable, yet gentle, breeze that caresses as it effects change. While not seen directly, its effects are evident with leaves moving, seeds spreading, ships given power and a weak bird given a much needed boost. This should describe our very lives as we are called to be known more for the lives we live than for the words we give. Someone once said that people will forget what you said but never how you made them feel. May we endeavor to be a gentle breeze in a world filled with raging storms; a breeze that soothes, cools, spreads and encourages the lives of those around us.

Soothing medicine: This speaks of a remedy that does not taste bad or create other issues and side effects, but one that heals with no bite. Not like the days when medicine was a leather belt and a shot of whiskey, but a soothing medicine that can't be stopped, gently caressing and effecting change. This world is sick and in need of a healing medicine. The sickness is sin, and the medicine is the gospel of Jesus Christ. And while we are to take that medicine to the sick, we are not to force it so aggressively down their throats that they turn away as a child would a spoonful of Ipecac syrup! Simple Mary Poppins practicality: "A spoonful of sugar helps the medicine go down"! Remember back to that person who shared Jesus with you? I would bet that they did not thump you in the head with the biggest King James Bible sold, shouting that unless you repented, you would burn for all eternity in a place called Hell! If I were a betting man, I would say that someone cared enough *about you* to build a relationship *with you* and, like a soothing medicine, they loved the cross *to you*.

A tamed wild animal: Lastly, and more accurately, this word "meek" in the original Greek language speaks of a young lion that was taken from the wild and raised and trained to be gentle—to be tamed. That is precisely what Jesus means when He says that we are to be meek: to be full of potential and power yet subdued and in control!

The best definition I have ever heard for meekness? Power under control.

So, the best definition I have ever heard for meekness? Power under control.

God has given us His power and the power to control that power. What power? The "gesture of a finger" power of God that was used in creation (Isaiah 40:12) and the "moving hand of God" power used to destroy creation (1 Chronicles 21:15).

The "parting of the waters" power of God that brought deliverance to the people of Egypt through Moses (Ex. 14:21) and the "closing in of the waters" power of God that brought destruction (Exodus 14:28).

The "resurrection of the dead" power of God (John 11:43). The "sealing up the heavens" power of God and the "opening up of the heavens" power of God (Revelation 11:6). The "causing of the blind to see, the deaf to hear, the dumb to talk and the lame to walk" power of God (Matthew 11:5).

The taking a bottle out of the hand and putting a Bible in it power of God. The taking a mouth of blasphemy and giving it a mouth of praise power of God. And the transforming the reproach in the community to a blessing of the community power of God.

That power is in us!

So, the question is, what do we *do* with that power? As the old adage says, with power comes great responsibility!

The Responsibility in Meekness—What It Does

So, now that we have established what meekness is, power under control, how do we employ it in our lives? Simply put, we are to be Gentle Giants. There are times in this life that we must be gentle and there are times that we must be giants. There are times we must be quiet, step down, be subdued and reserved, like a sweet old Granny in a rocking chair with a needle in one hand and yarn in the other.

Then there are times that we must be vocal and step up, be made known and proactive; when each of us must be a seasoned warrior on the battleground, with a sword in one hand and the Bible in the other.

The question is: when are we to be gentle and when are we to be a giant?

Be Gentle When It Comes to Your Feelings, Emotions and Pride

The founder of our faith, Jesus Christ, set the bar high, but He did not leave us in the dark as for what to do, for He was willing to demonstrate His expectations through His very life. I Peter 2:21–24 reveals that "because Christ also suffered for us, leaving us an example, that ye should follow his steps: Who did no sin, neither was guile found in his mouth: Who, when he was reviled, reviled not again; when he suffered, he threatened not; but committed himself to him that judgeth righteously..."

So, with Jesus Christ as our standard and example, we should be ashamed when we get all riled up when someone sits in our seat, the preacher doesn't shake our hand or the church doesn't go where we want on a mission trip. When it comes to your preferences, vision, dreams and goals, be gentle.

You don't need to be all giant all the time or all gentle all the time. God is not calling for that in our lives.

Be a Giant Against Sin and Falsehood

So, when should you be a giant? Be a giant when it comes to others and the truth. Like Jesus, as recorded in Matthew 21:12, when He went to the temple and found it had been turned from a house of prayer to a den of thieves; He flipped the tables and cast the moneychangers out! And yet, through all of that, He did not sin. Likewise, we are told that it is okay to be angry, just not to sin in that anger (Ephesians 4:26). When does Tom McCracken get angry and turn green? Tell me Jesus Christ is not the Son of God, that He was not born of a virgin, or that He did not physically rise from the grave and defeat death. Tell me the Bible is outdated gibberish written by a bunch of uneducated Bedouin tribesman, or that there is no such thing as a literal heaven or hell, or even that my Jesus did not die for everyone. That's when I become a giant!

Put me in the same room as the folks from the Freedom from Religion Foundation, the American Civil Liberties Union, or Planned Parenthood with those godless pagans trying to remove prayer, celebrate sin, and kill babies. That's when I become a giant!

Let me witness division in God's house, conflict between brothers and sisters in Christ, and I will show you what a modern-day Goliath looks like!

When I see a child who is abused, a lady who is hurt, a special-needs person who is mocked, a senior citizen who is taken advantage of, my giant comes out! If you mess with me, I should be gentle. But if you mess with others, doctrine and truth, I become a giant.

A few years ago, one of our church members, an 85-year-old senior, was at home in bed sleeping when someone put a ladder to her upstairs window, broke in, drug her out of bed, threw her to the ground, beat her, raped her and left her for dead. All I will say is that my church family, and community, saw the giant in me come out.

But, you don't need to be *all* giant all the time or *all* gentle all the time; God is not calling for that in our lives. It is all about balance, or using the power to control the power.

The Resources for Meekness—How It Is Done

So now you know what meekness is and when to use it. The question remains, how can we be meek? We all know how hard it is to love when hated, pray when persecuted and turn the other cheek when struck.

The key is found in Psalm 37, which is what Jesus was referring to with this specific beatitude. So, to understand how to be meek, we must understand the reference to Psalm 37. I find four ideals from this text that—if evident in our lives—will result in meekness:

Trust in God (vs. 5b)
"Trust also in him; and he shall bring it to pass."

If you are to be a Gentle Giant, using the power to control the power, you must learn to trust God completely. Understand that life will be hard, won't make sense, and, at times, can't be explained.

You must come to the place where you acknowledge that His ways are not your ways and His thoughts are not your thoughts. Getting to the place of spiritual maturity where you stop trying to figure out the mind of God and, instead, simply trust the heart of God. That you stop trying to figure out why God does what He does and simply trust that your Father knows what is best for your life.

To trust God so completely that no matter what is going on in your life, He is sufficient, satisfying and enough. As John Piper says, "God is most glorified in us when we are most satisfied in Him." It is all about making Romans 8:28 your life verse: "...we know that for those who love God all things work together for good, for those who are called according to his purpose." *[3]*

You see, people who trust in God are those who recognize that nothing will come into their life that hasn't first been filtered through the loving will of God for their life. Trust in God believes that nothing catches Him off guard or by surprise. Trust in God believes there is never a circumstance on earth that finds God pacing the halls of Glory, wringing His hands and wondering what to do next as He looks at the trials of your life.

Adrian Rogers once asked his congregation "Has it ever occurred to you that it has never occurred to God?"

Commit to God (vs. 5a)
"Commit thy way unto the LORD..."

The interesting nugget here is what I discovered through a Hebrew word study on the word "commit." It means to "roll," which has two implications.

First, it speaks of something precious being rolled up in a protective layer. This word gives the picture of a precious and valuable gem being rolled up in a sleeve of velvet and being placed in the security of a safe. So we, being precious and valuable in the eyes of God, are rolled up in His Son Jesus Christ and placed in the security of His right hand (John 10:28)!

Paul puts it this way: "whether Paul or Apollos or Cephas or the world or life or death or the present or the future—all are yours, and you are Christ's, and Christ is God's" (1 Corinthians 3:22).

This word can also speak of a stone that is rolling down a hill. While there may be small obstacles in the way of the stone, because of the steep slope, the stone eventually makes it to the bottom. We too can roll like a stone down the hills of this world. Because we are in Christ, we don't have to let this world get us down, but can roll with it, knowing that whatever obstacles we encounter, all things will work out through our love for Him.

You are rolled up in God so that you can roll in this world: making progress, passing by and through obstacles and not stopping by long enough to get caught up in a mess! Paul knew this truth, and that is why he reminded us to "press on toward the goal for the prize of the upward call of God in Christ Jesus" (Philemon 3:14).

Quiet Before God (vs. 7a)
"Rest in the LORD, and wait patiently for him..."

If you are like me, patience is NOT your strong point! At best, we are like that guy who went to the top of the mountain and prayed to God, "Lord, give me patience and give it to me now!"

In our current, instant and busy culture, patience and rest are needed more now than ever. If you are not careful, you will fill your schedule to the point that when you finally lay down for the night, if you're being honest, you must confess that there was no time in the day that you got still to know that God is God.

You might be thinking, "But I talk to God plenty; I bring Him all of my worries, troubles, fears, requests, petitions and prayers."

I am sure you do. But honestly, when was the last time you went into a prayer closet, turned off your phone, got quiet and just listened to Him speak to you for more than a few minutes?

I remember a project I was given when attending seminary at Liberty University. My professor asked us to turn off our phones and go into a closet, without a watch, and pray for 30 minutes. Well, I was rather presumptuous and cocky, and from the outset knew that as a pastor I would impress this guy with a paper that boasted at least an hour of prayer! Thirty minutes sounded so superficial; I mean, my sermons are justified at 45 minutes long because you can't communicate anything of importance in less time than that!

So, into the closet I went. I started praying for my family, then moved to my church family, then my neighborhood, the missionaries we support, the sick and afflicted, and then I gave time to be still and listen to what He wanted to say to me. After what I thought was at least an hour, I exited the closet, grabbed my watch and with a prideful look discovered I had been in that closet, in prayer, for a whole 20 minutes! We are just not used to being still and displaying patience.

What I have learned in the years since that project is that while it's great that I take time to speak to God, it is even greater still when I afford the time for Him to speak to me!

Do Not Fret for God (vs. 7b)
"Fret not thyself because of him who prospereth in his way, because of the man who bringeth wicked devices to pass."

The struggle with watching the evil prosper and the godly suffer has always been an issue with humanity. That is why God has made this issue easy for His children.

You see, we don't have to figure out who did wrong and what their judgment should be. We don't have to worry about making wrongs right and fixing that which is broken.

The message from Paul is: "Beloved, never avenge yourselves, but leave it to the wrath of God, for it is written, 'Vengeance is mine, I will repay, says the Lord'" (Romans 12:19). I know this may be offensive to you, but as much as you like doing and staying busy and helping God take care of business, God does not need your help! In fact, He does not want your help, for while we only see what people do, God sees why they do what they do, and that makes Him the only One qualified to serve as Judge.

So, to be meek you must trust and commit to God, be still before God and fret not for God.

The Rewards for Meekness—What It Gives
"Blessed are the meek, for they shall inherit the earth."
(Matthew 5:5)

We inherit the earth! I don't know about you, but I am looking at this reward and wondering, "Really? What I get for being meek is to inherit the earth?" Have you looked at this place lately? I mean, maybe before Adam and Eve ate from the tree and messed everything up! But now, there are thorns on the roses, dust in the air, animals wanting to eat humans, war, pestilence, sickness and disease. And don't even get me started on the earthquakes, typhoons, hurricanes, tornadoes and blizzards. So why does Jesus make inheriting the earth sound like such a reward? Well, actually, the reward is two-fold:

Rewards Now

To inherit the earth means we can have confidence that there is coming a day when Jesus Christ will fix everything broken and make all wrongs right. We can have confidence that as we look around and see the sinner celebrating in prosperity with the bigger house, the better job, the nicer car, we can be sure that it all belongs to our Father and our Father has given it all to us. Not now, but I assure you, it will be worth the wait.

Trust me, you'll get down and discouraged, and this world will say you are justified. And, I could join you down that path. I have an incurable kidney disease, high blood pressure, diverticulosis, high cholesterol, two herniated disks, two shoulders on schedule for extensive surgery, severe repressed migraine syndrome and I won't even mention the brown spots that keep popping up on my face. My face! Oh, I could get discouraged, but I choose to claim the peace, joy and power that come from the confidence I have that one day soon, either through the casket or the clouds, I will be in the presence of my King and there proclaim that it has been worth it all!

I heard the story of a janitor who worked at a seminary. One day he was sitting with his back against the basketball goal outside during his lunch break, reading the Bible. A theology professor who was walking to his next class noticed this janitor reading from the book of Revelation and asked, in a rather snobby tone, "Do you actually *understand* the meaning of what you are reading?" To which the janitor replied "Yes sir, Jesus is gonna win!" That is the gift of this text, the reason Jesus calls this a reward, for we find a confidence and assurance that comes from God in knowing how it all ends. A confidence and assurance, through faith, that rewards us now.

Rewards Later

I have confidence in the blessed hope. I have faith. But there is coming a day when I will be able to check my faith in for sight at the Gates of Glory. I will walk through those gates of pearl, dance on the streets of gold, touch the walls of jasper and jump up and down on a foundation of precious stone, enjoying that place of big doors and no mores while meeting the greats and the saints, as I make my way up to that mansion on the hilltop to claim my inheritance through Christ Jesus and to worship my God forever and ever.

And, let me say that for me, the future reward I am most looking forward to up there, that gives me hope and joy down here, is not what is in heaven as much as what is not.

There will be no more (Revelation 21:4):

- Trials: No more disease, sickness, pains and aches. In fact, there is coming a day when God will put every hospital, nursing home and funeral home out of business!

- Tears: No more weeping over a wayward child, an unsaved spouse, or the loss of a loved one. No more sleepless nights crying into the pillow, feeling misunderstood and unloved. One day God Himself will wipe every tear from our eyes.

- Temptations: For me, this is what I look forward to most about heaven, that not only will my worship be without deterioration, distraction and disruption, all of which tempt me to take my eyes off of Jesus, but that I will never again be in a position of yielding to temptation and hurting my Father's heart.

The meek inherit the earth—no wonder John was pleading for Christ to return soon. What a reward!

Blessed are the meek, for they shall inherit the earth.
— Matthew 5:4

CHAPTER FOUR

A Healthy Hunger

"Blessed are those who hunger and thirst for righteousness, for they shall be satisfied."
— *Matthew 5:6*

At the outset, there are a few issues that we need to address with this text, the first being the language in the words "hunger" and "thirst." An interpretation that more accurately reflects the original Greek meaning would read like: "Blessed are those who are hunger*ing* and thirst*ing* for righteousness."

This text is not speaking of a one-time event or a past occurrence, but a constant longing; a deep, insatiable, continuous craving for righteousness.

Many folks will never experience what it is really like to hunger and thirst because with many of us the only decision we have to make, in regard to food, is whether or not to supersize our next meal.

In 1987, I went through a period of time that provided me with the unique opportunity to appreciate the meaning behind this verse, for I had such a sense of hunger and thirst. I was stationed on the United States Coast Guard Cutter *Sweetbrier* out of Cordova, Alaska. The scope of duty for this ship and her crew was to provide search and rescue, aids to navigation, law enforcement patrols, and international intervention.

Jesus wants to get us to the point that we are hungering and thirsting to the degree that He is all that we think about.

Since our missions were carried out in the Prince William Sound and the Bering Sea, we all had to go through Cold Water Survival School, which included spending time on an uninhabited island.

We were dropped a couple hundred yards off the beach in our leaking "waterproof" Gumby suits and were required to swim to shore, get dry, establish a camp in our groups of four to six, build a shelter, conduct a perimeter search, compile resources and survive until we were "rescued" a couple of days later.

This training was designed to replicate either a sinking ship or man overboard scenario. And since these situations could not be prepared for, we were instructed not to bring anything with us that we would normally not have on our person during the course of an average day. Our group found out later that some of the other groups smuggled cans of tuna, lighters, knives and even tobacco onto the island. Our group followed the rules to the tee and had nothing but wet clothes that became stiff as boards during the night. In fact, I used my Gumby suit as part of the roof for my shelter!

Those who desire a relationship with God must come to the place in their lives where they need *a relationship with God.*

Toward the end of this training, I had drunk water from my wrung-out socks and ate the rotten flesh off a washed-up dead fish I found on a rock! I can tell you that for the first time in my life, I was really hungering and thirsting. I had gotten to the point that my entire focus was on finding something to eat and drink, and nothing else mattered.

That is the theme of this text. Jesus wants to get us to the point where we are hungering and thirsting to the degree that He is all that we think about, and that nothing else matters. He wants us to have a deep, insatiable, continuous craving for righteousness.

What are we to hunger and thirst for? Righteousness! What is righteousness? Well, it's really not that simple. In fact, scholars have debated this question as it pertains to this text for years. Some think this is speaking of:

Salvation Given to Us by God

That would seem to confirm the thought brought out in Matthew 5:3, which says, "Blessed are the poor in spirit for theirs is the kingdom of heaven." Those who desire a relationship with God must come to the place in their lives where they *need* a relationship with God.

This is desperation, a hungering and thirsting. The same hungering and thirsting that caused an entire congregation under the preaching of Jonathan Edwards to run down the aisle, grasp hold of the altar, and cry out for mercy, fearing that at any moment the floor would open up wide for hell to receive them.

The same hungering and thirsting that caused me to double-time down the aisle of a church in Massachusetts in 1990 under the full conviction of the Holy Spirit of God that I was a sinner in need of a Savior.

The same hungering and thirsting that has been experienced by multitudes who have grown weary and tired of never being satisfied, ultimately crying out to Jesus and discovering the joy that comes from burdens lifted, forgiveness offered and receiving a life full of purpose and meaning. So, salvation certainly seems to be a fitting interpretation of our word "righteousness."

Another thought of what this righteousness could be is:

Standing Given for Us Through Christ

Many scholars believe this hungering and thirsting to be eschatological in nature; that this righteousness causes us to look ahead and be confident through this life, knowing that there will be a time when our Father will return, fix everything broken and make everything that is wrong right. This interpretation of the text speaks more to *standing* than to salvation.

The older I get and the more I study, the more I realize the less I know! But, I know who Jesus is, what He did, where He is, and who I am because of it all—my position or standing. I know that there is coming a day when my heart will stop beating, my eyes will close, my breath will leave and those who are left behind will bury my body in the ground, throwing up a gravestone marking the place where many think it all ends. But meanwhile, up in heaven, there will be some rejoicing going on, for another sinner has come home. The angels will be swirling, the saints dancing, the greats shouting, my Savior standing, oh what a day, what a glorious day that will be!

And, knowing these things to be true, I am hungering and thirsting for that final day when the clouds are rolled back like a scroll, the trumpet shall resound and my Lord shall descend, even so it is well with my soul!

So, I can certainly see why some interpret this word to speak of our standing through Christ, yet still other theologians and scholars believe this righteousness speaks of:

Sanctification Given by Us for This World

This is where I settle down in the interpretation of the word "righteousness." Sanctification simply means, "to set apart for a special purpose," and the "process of becoming holy." And, boy, do we need more believers that have an insatiable hungering and thirsting for the things of God; to be more and more conformed to His image; to be set apart and becoming holy! You see, this is not a one-time event that takes place during salvation, but a process. This is why the Apostle Paul admonishes, in Romans 12:1–2, to *"present your bodies a living sacrifice, holy, acceptable unto God, which is your reasonable service. And be not conformed to this world: but be ye transformed by the renewing of your mind, that ye may prove what is that good, and acceptable, and perfect, will of God."* So, salvation comes *from* God, and sanctification comes *from* us. This is what it means to have a hungering and thirsting for righteousness.

And the result of not having a hungering and thirsting for righteousness is hypocrisy owned by a professing Christian; hence, someone with a desecrated testimony. Think back with me and remember when you first came into a relationship with Jesus Christ. If you were anything like me:

- You could not read and hear enough from the Word of God.

- You could not stay away from the house of God, coming every time the doors were opened, not imagining a time when your church family was meeting and you were not in the center of it all.

- You were telling everyone you met about the glorious transformation that had occurred in your life.

- You spent more time praying than watching TV.

- You were on committees, working with children, teaching youth, helping on church workdays, going on visitations, filling up the offering plate, planning that next mission trip, loving God and loving people!

- You were so consumed for the things of God, obsessed with the Word of God and in desperate love with the people of God, that it was like you could never get enough, that your cup was constantly running over.

That is what it means, hungering and thirsting for righteousness. Gypsy Smith, a great evangelist in the early twentieth century, was once asked for the secret of his powerful and lasting ministry, to which he replied, "I never lost the wonder of it all." Never getting over your salvation or losing the wonder of it all is the meaning behind our hungering and thirsting for righteousness.

Tragically, so many Christians who used to be in the race are now in the ditch of life, no longer hungering and thirsting for righteousness.

Oh, friend, the need for you to hunger and thirst after righteousness is much bigger than you! Yes, God will bless *you* if you are hungering and thirsting after Him, but know this: you are not an island, and your life does affect those around you.

David knew this concept, which is why he was hungering and thirsting after righteousness and known as a man after God's own heart. There are certainly benefits to having an insatiable appetite for the things of God.

But here is the warning: When you cease to hunger and thirst after righteousness, you desecrate your testimony, trade power for hypocrisy and become gospel-useless. And when that happens, you lose joy, power, peace and victory in your life, at best, and become the excuse others use to reject the gospel of Jesus Christ, at worst.

Christians have unintentionally steered others away from Christ by starting more religions and cults than anyone else.

In the sixth century, a young man was born into this world, his dad dying before he was born and his mom dying when he was but seven years old. He was then raised by his grandfather, who also died and left him in the care of his uncle.

In spite of this dysfunctional and unstable background, he became a young man of great reputation: honest, hardworking, driven and passionate. He would go off every year in isolation to a cave, praying and fasting from sunup till sundown. It was during one of these trips that an "angel" came to him, declared him a messenger of God and told him to start a new religion. He ran home scared and told his wife and family to cover him for protection.

When he questioned this "angel's" message from God, for him to become a messenger and start a new religion, his wife brought him to her cousin, who was known as a Christian savant, someone who had a reputation for being informed and educated in Christianity. This "Christian" confirmed his calling, declared him to be a true prophet of God and encouraged him to start a new religion. This religion is now the second-largest religion in the world. I am talking about Islam and its founder, Muhammad.

In 1869, Mahatma Gandhi was born in India and eventually became a leader and voice of the third-largest world religion, Hinduism. Had he been exposed to genuine Christianity, he would have had the potential to influence and convert millions. In fact, there was a time in his life that he researched and investigated other religions, ultimately embracing some aspects of another religion, Sikhism. After his research, this is what he stated of Christianity: "I like your Christ; I do not like your Christians. Your Christians are so unlike your Christ."

In 1930, a very intelligent man was born in Chicago. He had a troubled upbringing, dropped out of high school, ran away and joined the carnival. He was exposed to, and even considered, many religions, even dabbling in the occult; he was what we would call a seeker. He was drawn more to Christianity than to any other religion and even started playing the organ for traveling preachers on Sundays at the carnival where he worked. Of Christianity he writes, "On Saturday night I would see men lusting after half-naked girls dancing at the carnival, and on Sunday morning when I was playing the organ for tent-show evangelists at the other end of the carnival lot, I would see these same men sitting in the pew with their wives and children, asking God to forgive them and purge them of carnal desires. And the next Saturday night they'd be back at the carnival or some other place of indulgence. I knew then that the Christian Church thrives on hypocrisy, and that man's carnal nature will win out!" Disillusioned and frustrated with the blatant hypocrisy thriving in Christianity, he decided to write a book and start his own church. His name was Anton LaVey; the book he wrote was the Satanic bible; and the church he started was the church of Satan. [4]

That is why I stated that Christians have unintentionally started more religions and cults than anyone else has.

But, not all cases are as blatant and apparent. What about the "Christian" parent who is more committed to sports on the Sabbath than to church? Or the "Christian" who honks and yells their way through traffic while displaying a fish magnet on their car? Or the employee who tells inappropriate jokes around the water cooler, gossips about their demanding boss, complains about every pain and ache, yet sings in their church choir every Sunday?

While not seemingly as destructive as writing a satanic bible, are these not examples of "Christians" who point people away from Christ by lives that declare Jesus is not enough?

What would this world be like if more Christians were hungering and thirsting after righteousness? What would *you* be like if you were hungering and thirsting after righteousness?

Satisfaction Given in Us Through the Holy Spirit

This is the message humanity needs so desperately to hear today. When you hunger and thirst for Christ, He will fill you! This world does not get this. Oh, there are many who are hungering and thirsting today, just not for the right things.

We hunger and thirst for things like drugs, relationships, alcohol, family, hobbies, education, money, approval, health, vanity, position, careers, food, power, praise and pleasure. Never forget: God designed us to have a hungering and a thirsting. He placed eternity in our hearts; it's in our very DNA! This is not new. Nor is it new for humanity to hunger and thirst after something other than God.

Satan was hungering and thirsting to rise into the heavens and become God. God humbled him. This was a hunger and thirst for *power* that was never satisfied.

King Nebuchadnezzar looked down at the great kingdom of Babylon and declared, "Is this not Babylon the great, which I myself have built as a royal residence by the might of my power and for the glory of my majesty?" (Daniel 4:30). God humbled him. This was a hunger and thirst for *praise* that was never satisfied.

The story of the rich young fool, as taught by Jesus, depicted a man who thought life was summed up in the statement "eat, drink and be merry" (Luke 12:19). God humbled him. This was a hunger and thirst for *pleasure* that was never satisfied.

As I look at the above examples of a life hungering and thirsting after things like power, praise and pleasure, I recognize there was a time when this was descriptive of my life. I remember clearly a few months before I became a follower of Christ that I had this overwhelming sense of a void in my life. After one long night of tossing and turning, I got out of bed, grabbed a piece of paper and a pencil and took an inventory of my life. When I finished, everything appeared to be good, yet I still felt there was something missing, an undetermined and unrecognized void. I had power, praise and pleasure, yet unexplainably remained unsatisfied. It was only after I came to Christ that I discovered what true satisfaction was.

In attacking the prosperity gospel, John Piper has pointed out that even if we are involved in a car accident that flings our child through the windshield to die in a pool of blood on the street, Jesus Christ can be enough. That is why we should hunger and thirst after righteousness, as it is only through this act that we can be satisfied, completely satisfied, no matter what. *[5]*

"Blessed are those who hunger and thirst for righteousness, for they shall be satisfied."
— ***Matthew 5:6***

CHAPTER FIVE

Compassion in Action

Blessed are the merciful, for they shall receive mercy.
— Matthew 5:7

While the first four beatitudes deal with our relationship with God, these next four deal with our relationships with each other. This is where so many professing Christians are missing the mark.

Many think they can have a great relationship with God and never make the connection with other believers or even His church.

To understand these beatitudes is to understand that what God gives us is not meant to be kept to ourselves, but given out to others! Christianity is an outpouring of an indwelling. So, through the beatitudes, we find that we have been given eternal life, comfort, power and satisfaction, and the first thing that God tells us to do with these glorious gifts is to show mercy.

Mercy Is Foreign to the World and Will Not Be Rewarded by the World

In the Roman culture in which this sermon was given, mercy was not a popular concept to better society, but rather a weakness to be eradicated. One Roman philosopher called mercy "the disease of the soul." It was in this setting that when a child was born, the baby would be lifted up to the father and if he thought the child was healthy and attractive, he would give a "thumbs up" and the child would live. If he thought the child ugly, too loud or unhealthy, he would give a "thumbs down" and the child would be put to death.

And in this merciless culture a Roman citizen, for any reason, could kill and bury a slave without any consequence. Additionally, a husband could put his wife to death without fear of retribution.

It was in this dark culture, void of mercy, that Jesus stated, "Blessed are the merciful, for they shall receive mercy." Not much has changed from the culture of Roman history to our current American culture as we are giving a "thumbs down" to 1.2 million unborn babies each year in America and calling it abortion.

Domestic violence is the leading cause of injury to women between the ages of 15 and 44 in the United States, more than car accidents, muggings and rapes combined.

Mercy has always been foreign to the world and not rewarded by the world. Jesus made the lame to walk again, and He caused the blind to see. He brought the dead to life and hearing to the deaf, and reached out to the outcasts and the untouchables. He sought out the tax collectors, the degenerates, the immoral, the prostitutes, the drunkards, the despised and the rejected, and praise God, He even reached out to the likes of you and me!

Jesus shocked the culture of the day by His many displays of great mercy, and those acts of mercy were rarely received with gratefulness but often rejected with hostility. He was shamed, had stones thrown at Him and was accused of being demon-possessed, drunk and crazy. And yet, He never stopped.

Jesus showed us by example that mercy is foreign to the world and rejected by the world. If they rejected Jesus and His mercy, they will reject you and your mercy.

> *If the world hates you, know that it has hated me before it hated you.*
> — *John 15:18*

Yet, we must continue to be agents of mercy to those around us if we are to receive mercy from the Father above us.

Mercy Is Not a Feeling but Compassion in Action

The *Preaching the Word* commentary on Matthew explains this "compassion in action" principle by the story of a nineteenth-century preacher who happened across a friend whose horse had just been accidentally killed. [6]

While a crowd of onlookers expressed empty words of sympathy, the preacher stepped forward and said to the loudest sympathizer, "I am sorry five pounds. How much are you sorry?" And then he passed the hat. True mercy demands action. True mercy always translates to action; this is compassion in action.

Let's break this "compassion in action" down to three areas: *meeting right physical needs, holding a right attitude* and *being spiritually mature.*

Meeting the Right Physical Needs

Notice I qualified this idea of meeting physical needs with the use of the word "right." We are not called to enable the greedy but to empower the needy. To feed the hungry, visit the sick, provide for the orphans and widows, clothe the naked and visit the imprisoned. Yet, not all people seeking help should receive the specific help requested. Years ago I was standing in line at a local restaurant after church with some friends waiting for a table. We were approached by a clearly homeless man who was seeking money for "food." Wanting to set the pastoral example before other Christians, I obliged and gave the man a twenty-dollar bill. He happily took my money, and I was feeling pretty good about this deed until my eyes followed this man right to the liquor store across the street! I left that restaurant, crossed the street and found him at the counter with a fifth of whiskey, handing the clerk my twenty-dollar bill. Needless to say, I left him penniless at the counter! While we are to meet the needs of those around us, as best we can with the resources God has provided, we must qualify those needs with the wisdom and discernment God has given. Again, we are not called to enable the greedy but to empower the needy.

Holding a Right Attitude

John MacArthur, in his commentary on Matthew, states: "Mercy does not hold a grudge, harbor resentment, capitalize on another's failure or weakness, or publicize another's sin. On a great table at which he fed countless hundreds of people, Augustine inscribed, 'Whoever thinks that he is able to nibble at the life of absent friends, must know that he's unworthy of this table.' The vindictive, heartless, and indifferent are not subjects of Christ; they show they have passed Christ's kingdom. When they pass need by on the other side, as the priest and the Levite did in the story of the Good Samaritan, they show they have passed Christ by." [7]

While it is crucial that we are found faithful in being merciful, we must always be certain that we are as faithful in having a right attitude. So many times we have an ulterior motive or personal agenda behind our acts of mercy. While we may be showing mercy, we must be sure that our good deeds are not for recognition, worldly reward or human reciprocation, but for the glory of our Father and for Him alone.

Being Spiritually Mature

This aspect is broken down into three parts: *pity, provocation and prayer*, all of which involve God's children doing more than just crying out, losing sleep or even feeling bad—again highlighting the truth that mercy is much more than a feeling or emotion. Mercy, true mercy, always fleshes out as action, which comes from spiritual maturity.

Mercy Is Shown Through Pity

Augustine stated, "If I weep for the body from which the soul is departed, should I not weep for the soul from which God is departed?"

I have been to hundreds of funerals, and if memory serves correctly, every one of them, without exception, involved people crying over the body of someone who died. Mercy is displayed in the believer's life when they cry more for those who will be missed in heaven than those they miss on earth. Mercy is shown through pity.

Mercy Is Shown Through Provocation

I believe many do not come to church because they are living in sin and the minister, the music and the membership all represent God, and that means conflict.

The greatest mercy you can show to someone is presenting them with the gospel. By not showing mercy through provocation, you could be securing their fate of eternal separation from the only hope they have! Be bold, be passionate, be proactive, be conflicting, be offensive, be whatever you need to be to get their attention on their sin so that they can bring that sin to the attention of the Savior.

Mercy Is Shown Through Prayer

MacArthur gauges it this way: "Our mercy can be measured by our prayer for the unsaved and for Christians who are walking in disobedience."

This goes back to Matthew 5:4: "Blessed are those who mourn, for they shall be comforted." Mourn over what? Your sin and the sins of those around you. When was the last time you really cried out in prayer for the lost and the disobedient, knowing they were hurting the very heart of God?

Oh, how far we have come in American church culture. There was a time when the church would gather every Wednesday night, collapse at the altar and cry out in prayer for the unsaved and the backslidden.

Wood was warped and carpet stained as the mourning of congregations resonated within the sanctuary of God.

We need some more old-fashioned church services where mercy is shown through prayer. We need some old-school, confession-and-repentance time of prayer where we are getting right with God and each other and, through the power of unity, getting this world back to a right relationship with God.

As recorded in 2 Chronicles 7:14, "If my people who are called by my name humble themselves, and pray and seek my face and turn from their wicked ways, then I will hear from heaven and will forgive their sin and heal their land." This world is sick and in need of healing, and we have the cure! The answer is not to be found in the school house, court house, police house and certainly not the White House, but in God's house, with His people revealing a merciful God by being merciful.

Mercy Is Anchored to Forgiveness Rooted in Christ

Mercy is anchored to forgiveness rooted in Christ. When I fell at the cross 24 years ago, I was a wicked, vile, worldly, self-consumed, and flesh-driven sinner, deserving of jail in this life and hell in the next. And the truth is, I am still that sinner. I am just fortunate enough to have experienced the forgiveness of a Holy God through a loving Savior! I am not better than those who are still in the darkness of their sin, but I am better off!

I am better off because I have received the mercy, love and forgiveness offered by Jesus Christ and have been made His child forever.

I can think of no better illustration that mercy is anchored to forgiveness than the story of Corrie ten Boom. In an excerpt from her book, *The Hiding Place,* Corrie relates the following story:

"It was in a church in Munich that I saw him—a balding, heavyset man in a gray overcoat, a brown felt hat clutched between his hands. People were filing out of the basement room where I had just spoken, moving along the rows of wooden chairs to the door at the rear. It was 1947 and I had come from Holland to defeated Germany with the message that God forgives.

"It was the truth they needed most to hear in that bitter, bombed-out land, and I gave them my favorite mental picture. Maybe because the sea is never far from a Hollander's mind, I liked to think that that's where forgiven sins were thrown. 'When we confess our sins,' I said, 'God casts them into the deepest ocean, gone forever....'

"The solemn faces stared back at me, not quite daring to believe. There were never questions after a talk in Germany in 1947. People stood up in silence, in silence collected their wraps, in silence left the room.

"And that's when I saw him, working his way forward against the others. One moment I saw the overcoat and the brown hat; the next, a blue uniform and a visored cap with its skull and crossbones. It came back with a rush: the huge room with its harsh overhead lights; the pathetic pile of dresses and shoes in the center of the floor; the shame of walking naked past this man. I could see my sister's frail form ahead of me, ribs sharp beneath the parchment skin. Betsie, how thin you were!

[Betsie and I had been arrested for concealing Jews in our home during the Nazi occupation of Holland; this

man had been a guard at Ravensbruck concentration camp where we were sent.]

"Now he was in front of me, hand thrust out: 'A fine message, Fräulein! How good it is to know that, as you say, all our sins are at the bottom of the sea!'

"And I, who had spoken so glibly of forgiveness, fumbled in my pocketbook rather than take that hand. He would not remember me, of course—how could he remember one prisoner among those thousands of women?

"But I remembered him and the leather crop swinging from his belt. I was face-to-face with one of my captors and my blood seemed to freeze.

"'You mentioned Ravensbruck in your talk,' he was saying, 'I was a guard there.' No, he did not remember me.

"'But since that time,' he went on, 'I have become a Christian. I know that God has forgiven me for the cruel things I did there, but I would like to hear it from your lips as well. Fräulein,' again the hand came out—'will you forgive me?'

"And I stood there—I whose sins had again and again to be forgiven—and could not forgive. Betsie had died in that place—could he erase her slow terrible death simply for the asking?

"It could not have been many seconds that he stood there—hand held out—but to me it seemed hours as I wrestled with the most difficult thing I had ever had to do.

"For I had to do it—I knew that. The message that God forgives has a prior condition: that we forgive those who have injured us. 'If you do not forgive men their trespasses,' Jesus says, 'neither will your Father in heaven forgive your trespasses.'

"I knew it not only as a commandment of God, but as a daily experience. Since the end of the war I had had a home in Holland for victims of Nazi brutality. Those who were able to forgive their former enemies were able also to return to the outside world and rebuild their lives, no matter what the physical scars. Those who nursed their bitterness remained invalids. It was as simple and as horrible as that.

"And still I stood there with the coldness clutching my heart. But forgiveness is not an emotion—I knew that too. Forgiveness is an act of the will, and the will can function regardless of the temperature of the heart. '... Help!' I prayed silently. 'I can lift my hand. I can do that much. You supply the feeling.'

"And so woodenly, mechanically, I thrust my hand into the one stretched out to me. And as I did, an incredible thing took place. The current started in my shoulder, raced down my arm, sprang into our joined hands. And then this healing warmth seemed to flood my whole being, bringing tears to my eyes.

"'I forgive you, brother!' I cried. 'With all my heart!'

"For a long moment we grasped each other's hands, the former guard and the former prisoner. I had never known God's love so intensely, as I did then." [8]

If we have received unmerited forgiveness from God, then we must give that forgiveness freely to others. For the truth is, it is not our mercy we are to keep; it is His mercy we are to give.

Mercy Is Rewarded by the Faithfulness of God

Blessed are the merciful, for they shall receive mercy.
— Matthew 5:7

This is the only beatitude that speaks of getting what you give. Not from the world, but from God! If you show mercy, you will receive mercy. What does this mean? The other beatitudes seem pretty clear: when we are poor in spirit, we receive the kingdom of heaven. When we mourn, we receive comfort. When we display meekness, we inherit the earth. And when we hunger and thirst for righteousness, we are promised to be filled. But show mercy and receive mercy? This means that you will benefit from the faithfulness of God.

If you allow God to demonstrate His mercy through you *by showing mercy to those* around you, *you will receive mercy from the One* above you *by His assurance* within you.

You see, when you show mercy, you are demonstrating that you have a power within that can only come from without. Hence, we are able to experience a two-fold blessing:

An Internal Blessing

Assurance of salvation: This is a promise from God, friend; a promise that can change your life. Showing mercy is an indication that you are saved and secure so that you can be sure.

Do you have days that you doubt? Days you struggle? Nights when you wonder if God has left you, forgotten you, given up on you? Times when your feelings seem to trump your beliefs?

If you allow God to demonstrate His mercy *through you* by showing mercy to those *around you*, you will receive mercy from the One *above you* by His assurance *within you.*

There is no higher joy and no better comfort than being able to lay down at night—even in the midst of the doubting and accusing voices from the world, the devil and even the flesh—only to have a text like this penetrate that doubt with the wonderful truth that you are His and He is yours!

An External Blessing

Access to salvation: This world needs the joy and comfort that you have received from God. And in this merciless culture in which we live, there is no greater stage on which to present the gospel than through mercy shown to those in need. One of my favorite contemporary Christian artists, For King & Country, released a song in 2014 entitled "Fix My Eyes." The words of that song speak an incredible blessing to this truth.

The truth is, as believers, we all have the unique opportunity to display mercy to those around us by letting out what is in us, for the glory of the One above us, that all would come to the saving knowledge of the One who died for all of us.

And, before we move on, let me add a warning never to replace inviting people to Christ with inviting people to church. I truly believe that we need to focus less on inviting people to church and focus more on inviting people to become the church. Showing mercy is giving people what they need, and what people need the most is help from the only One able to help—not a church and not a religion. People need the Lord.

Blessed are the merciful, for they shall receive mercy.
— ***Matthew 5:7***

CHAPTER SIX

Pure Is More

Blessed are the pure in heart, for they shall see God.
— *Matthew 5:8*

Kent Hughes, in his commentary on the Sermon on the Mount, relates the story of Anna Mae Pennica, a 62-year-old woman who had been blind since birth. At age 47 she married a man she met in Braille class *[9]*; and for the first fifteen years of their marriage, he did the seeing for both of them until he completely lost his vision to retinitis pigmentosa.

Mrs. Pennica had never seen the green of spring or the blue of a winter sky. Yet, because she had grown up in a loving, supportive family, she never felt resentful about her handicap and always exuded a remarkably cheerful spirit.

Then in October 1981, Dr. Thomas Pettit of the Jules Stein Eye Institute of the University of California at Los Angeles performed surgery to remove the rare congenital cataracts from the lens of her left eye and Mrs. Pennica saw for the first time ever!

She found that everything was "so much bigger and brighter" than she ever imagined. While she immediately recognized her husband and others that she had known well, other acquaintances were taller or shorter, heavier or skinnier than she had pictured them.

Oh, how many graces of God we often take for granted.

Since that day, Mrs. Pennica has hardly been able to wait to wake up in the morning, splash her eyes with water, put on her glasses and enjoy the changing morning light. Her vision is almost 20/30, good enough to pass a driver's test!

Can you even imagine? Oh, how many graces of God we often take for granted. Think what it must have been like to live for many years not seeing and then being able to watch the sunrise for the very first time? To enjoy the sunset on the ocean as birds fly by? Or to gaze into the eyes of your lover, wink at your child or watch a football game?

Seeing is glorious; it is a miracle, really.

There are three truths that stick out to me as I consider our text: *a devotion to purity, the depth of purity,* and *our desire for purity.*

A Devotion to Purity

First of all, what is purity? The original root Greek word used here for purity conveyed several meanings: removing bacteria from water and alloy from metal, getting rid of unmixed feelings to achieve clarity and banishing evil in order to enjoy freedom.

So, purity would be getting to the point in your life where you have achieved clarity and focus on the things of God by banishing evil from your life, in order to enjoy the freedom in Christ that He longs for you to have.

> *When we fall in love with Jesus Christ, our lives are marked by that kind of love.*

Do this and you will be assured a power-filled, victorious Christian life that will make a difference *in* this world by bringing the glory of God *to* this world!

I know what you are thinking, "You don't know the boss I have to work for, the issues we are battling at home, or the pain I experience every day of my life."

Wouldn't most of us like to put all of those things on the altar, kill them, put them in a locked box, bury them deep in the ground, and be able to walk away and live for Christ unhindered?

That is exactly what the Bible tells us to do every day! Galatians 5:24 says, "And those who belong to Christ Jesus have crucified the flesh with its passions and desires."

That means you have to get to the point where Matthew 5:4—"Blessed are those who mourn, for they shall be comforted"—is prevalent in your life! When we fall in love with Jesus Christ, our lives are marked by that kind of love. And when He hurts, we hurt. And what hurts Him the most is when our disobedience, our sin, stops our lives from bringing Him glory. So, we must get angry at our sin, take it out to the woodshed and beat it down, standing over it and declaring, "Today I will be serving my Lord and there is no room for you!" then turn around and walk away in victory.

D. L. Moody attended a revival one night and heard the evangelist make this statement: "The world has yet to see what God can do with a man fully consecrated to him."

Later, Moody travelled back to the States, and when he took that first step off the ship onto the dock, he repeated that line: "The world has yet to see what God can do with a man fully consecrated to him." And then he added, "By God's help, I aim to be that man."

You see, we are not the only ones who desire to be that man, woman, boy or girl, and we are not the only ones who struggle in making it happen.

Even after a church service on a Sunday morning when we get a taste of glory—the sermon is powerful, the music inspirational, and the prayers and fellowship sweet—it does not take long to realize how weak we are, for even on our way home, the moment someone cuts us off in traffic and gives a hand gesture that does not mean we are number one, we lose it. How then? How can we remain pure and experience a close, intimate and powerful relationship with God in this flesh, surrounded by the darkness of this world? I believe the answer is found in the kind of purity to which we have a devotion. There are six types of purity:

Primal Purity

This is a purity held only by God. Hinduism, the third-largest religion, tells of their god, Shiva, who is living on a holy mountain in Asia, doing Yoga, smoking marijuana and having sex—and millions worship him! Thank God that our God is pure! What does it mean that our God is pure? It means:

- He is mercy, justice and love.

- He will never go back on His word.

- He will never get so fed up with you that He takes out His eraser and blots your name out of the heavenly roll.

- His love never fails, never gives up and never runs out.

- Nothing catches Him off guard or by surprise.

- It means there will *never* be a time when you can look up into heaven and find God pacing the halls of glory, wringing His hands, wondering what to do next because He did not see *that* coming!

- He knows you better than anyone, yet chooses to love you more than everyone.

It means when this life is over, and you get to glory and see God face-to-face, He will be everything and more than you have ever read or heard about Him; and on that day you will declare that it has been worth it all. That is primal purity.

Created Purity

This was the purity enjoyed by Adam and Eve before the fall. Being able to walk and talk with God through the garden without temptation or distraction. They were able to look into the eyes of God without fear and live free of guilt. This purity was lost when Adam and Eve chose to rebel and sin against God.

Positional Purity

This is the purity achieved through salvation. When we make that decision to "confess with our mouths that Jesus is Lord and believe in our hearts that God raised him from the dead" (Romans 10:9), we become pure in position. In other words, as dark, evil, wicked and unworthy as you are, after salvation, when you stand before God, He no longer sees that sin, but sees His Son, our Savior!

Imputed or Actual Purity

This is the purity spoken of by Paul when he stated in 2 Corinthians 5:17, "Therefore if any man be in Christ, he is a new creature: old things are passed away: behold, all things are become new." I love this text. I can now go back to my family and friends, who knew me before I met Christ, and say, "Remember that sinful, rebellious and angry Tom that you used to know? The one that you tossed aside and predicted would end up dead or in jail? The one that you said would never make anything of himself? Well, have I got something to show you now; behold, all things have become new! Come and see the great things that Christ has done!" I love the way the Apostle Paul put it when he said that we are to "put on the Lord Jesus Christ" (Romans 13:14a). Now that I am wearing the righteousness of Jesus, I can declare that His righteousness looks pretty good on me! This is imputed, or actual, purity.

Practical Purity

This is how purity is played out in the everyday, mundane, routine life of the believer. This is the purity to which we need a devotion. It is also called *sanctification*. We need a devotion to setting our lives apart for the glorious purpose of making Christ known to this world through a life dedicated and consecrated to, through and for Him.

Ultimate Purity

This is the heavenly purity that all born-again believers will one day enjoy. This is the aspect of salvation that I am most looking forward to, although there are many aspects to heaven that the collective church celebrates in anticipation while on earth: the streets of gold, walls of jasper, foundation of precious stone and the gates of pearl; the angelic beings, the greats and the saints, the family and friends that are missed and the lives that were touched but remain unknown to us this side of eternity.

Ultimate purity goes much deeper than any of these things. Ultimate purity brings us into an aspect of our salvation that we have yet to experience: freedom from the confines of this sinful body! Freedom to focus on Jesus Christ, giving Him unadulterated worship from a completely pure heart of integrity, with no distractions, disruptions or deteriorations. A future where we will be able to walk and talk with Him with complete focus, free of shame, guilt and fear. That is heaven! The Garden of Eden restored and the curse cured! And that is the ultimate purity we will one day enjoy; but for now, our devotion needs to be aimed at practical purity.

Most scholars believe that Jesus is pulling from Psalm chapter 24:3–4, where David declared: "Who shall ascend into the hill of the Lord? Or who shall stand in his holy place? He that hath clean hands, and a pure heart; who hath not lifted up his soul unto vanity, nor sworn deceitfully."

Who can ascend into the hill of the Lord or stand in His holy place? Those with clean hands and a pure heart! If you desire more from your relationship with God, you must realize the scope of this purity, or:

The Depth of Purity

Although works are important in the believer's life, remember the verse: "Blessed are the merciful for they shall receive mercy"? We must clothe the naked, feed the hungry and provide for the orphans and widows, remembering that God has not called us to enable the greedy, but to empower the needy. Having clean hands is not enough; those clean hands, or works, must come from a pure heart.

Simply put, while other books may speak to us, the Word of God has the ability to speak through us. It is the only book that is supernatural, as it was breathed by God, so it is alive, active, full of energy and power and able to discern not just the things people do, but also why they do the things they do!

The depth that I am speaking to here is to go past the *what* and focus on the *why*. To go deeper than what we are doing and hone in on why we do what we do. How is this done? Through the Word of God:

"For the word of God is living and active, sharper than any two-edged sword, piercing to the division of the soul and of spirit, of joints and of marrow, and discerning the thoughts and intentions of the heart" (Hebrews 4:12).

Simply put, while other books may speak to us, the Word of God has the ability to speak *through* us. It is the only book that is supernatural, as it was breathed by God, so it is alive, active, full of energy and power and able to discern not just the things people do, but also why they do the things they do!

What drives, motivates, and compels you? The Word of God has the power to recognize the outside actions and reveal the inward attitudes.

> *I am with John Stott when he declared, "The less the preacher comes between the Word and its hearers, the better."*

This is why I am so thankful for my church, where the Word of God is at the core of all that we do. So many who come through the doors of CommUNITY Church proclaim that the one very evident thing about our church is the importance of the Word of God. I am with John Stott when he declared, "The less the preacher comes between the Word and its hearers, the better." And with Charles Spurgeon when he stated, "No man who preaches the gospel without zeal is sent from God to preach at all."

Oh, while I might have some great things to say, teach and preach based on my experience and education, only God's Word has the supernatural ability to change lives.

And, for the Child of God who is walking in the will of God, engaged in the work of God and studying the Word of God, this two-edged sword, or truer to the original language, "surgeon's scalpel," is quite the blessing! Because the Holy Spirit speaks through the Word of God and is able to know your thoughts like no one else, understand what you are feeling like no one else, hear your silent cries like no one else and see those internal struggles like no one else, the Word of God is able to bring you comfort, peace, joy, love, power and victory like no one else.

It is through the Word that we can achieve this depth of purity. That is why a preacher at a men's conference I attended a few years ago kept shouting, "Get your head in the bread!"

So, what then? It should all boil down to:

Our Desire for Purity

Why should we seek purity? What happens to the owner of a pure heart? You see God!

I remember my salvation as if it happened yesterday. Sitting in the very back of that church so that I could arrive last and leave first; in and out, just checking church attendance off of my "to do" list. Then something unexpected happened to me:

"Heaven came down and glory filled my soul, when at the cross the Savior made me whole, my sins were

washed away and my night was turned to day, Heaven came down and glory filled my soul." [10]

I will never forget leaving that sanctuary that day! As I walked outside, it was as if God had repainted the landscape of the world: trees looked greener, the sky bluer, the sun brighter and my burdens lighter. From that moment on, I could see God!

- I see Him in the gentle breeze on a spring day.

- I see Him in every tree that seems to be reaching up to the sky in praise to the Creator.

- I see Him in the ant crawling on the ground and in the bird flying in the sky.

- I see Him in the bright eyes of a newborn baby.

- I see Him in the lonely gaze held by the wheelchair-bound senior in the nursing home, looking for Christ and longing for home.

In my life now, everything and everyone I see reminds me of a gloriously powerful and loving God who creates and sustains all life.

Praise God that I can see Him now, but greater still that I will see Him even more clearly later. The Apostle Paul speaks of this "seeing God," for he states in 1 Corinthians 13:12, "For now we see in a mirror dimly, but then face to face. Now I know in part; then I shall know fully, even as I have been fully known."

One day we will check in our faith for sight and see God face-to-face! Oh, what a day that will be! What sight we will have!

Think bigger than the streets of gold, the walls of jasper, the foundation of precious stone, the gates of pearl. Look beyond the friends and family enjoying their new bodies, and the greats and saints from the Bible. Go deeper than the peaceful, still river and the tree of life replanted in the Garden of Tomorrow, described in the book of Revelation.

For eternity you will be able to gaze into the eyes of the One who set you free and loved you with an everlasting love with a clear focus, not tainted by the effects of sin or ravished by age. Finally, for the first time in your life, you will be able to see, really see, your Savior and Father, Jesus Christ. Now *that* is quite the reward for having a pure heart; that is purity worth desiring.

Having a heart that is pure and being rewarded with seeing God is so pleasurable and life-changing that nothing else even compares.

That being said, tragically, there are many times that I have traded that kind of supernatural, heavenly pleasure for the brief, temporal and hollow pleasures of this world. Remember 62-year-old Mrs. Pennica? According to her "miracle" eye surgeon doctor, surgical techniques available as far back as the 1940s could have corrected her problem. Don't miss this: Mrs. Pennica lived 40 of her 62 sightless years needlessly blind.

Perhaps you do not have the joy, comfort and power that come from a pure heart because you have never taken that first step of being poor in spirit.

That is the thought brought out in our Christian anthem "Amazing Grace": "I once was lost but now I am found, was blind but now I see."

Please let me introduce you to the Great Physician, who has been performing the same sight-saving procedure for over 2000 years with a 100-percent success rate. His name is Jesus.

And, once you have this step and set your sights on being pure in heart, then you will be able to see God in a more intimate and personal way than ever before!

This is the difference between "seeing is believing" and "believing is seeing." Let me explain. When I was 21 years old and searching for answers, I was operating under the "seeing is believing" mentality of the world. I remember being in a hotel room, opening the nightstand drawer and removing the Gideon Bible. I was at the end of my rope, feeling lost, desperate for answers and wanted so badly for God to show Himself, that I might believe.

In fact, I took that Bible out and called out to God, "If you are really there, open this Bible and I will follow you forever." The Bible remained closed. So, I struck another deal. "God," I said, "I will open it for you, just let me open it to a page where it talks about how much you care for me." I forget what page I turned to, but I was still left without my specific request being fulfilled. In a last plea I asked God to make one of the cars on the highway honk a horn in the next sixty seconds, and that alone would cause me to follow Him. Nothing but silence for the next hour!

It was six months later when I called out to Him from my sin and asked Him to be the Lord of my life before I realized the truth. While the world is all about "seeing is believing," faith changes that up with "believing is seeing." For once I came by faith to Him, I saw more clearly than ever before. And in the years since, as I focus on being pure in heart, I have found new aspects of His glory every single day! I have been in a relationship with Him for 24 years, and I am still learning about Him and growing in Him.

I hope today that you understand the devotion to purity and the depth of purity so that you have an insatiable desire for purity—to understand that pure is more.

Blessed are the pure in heart, for they shall see God.
— *Matthew 5:8*

CHAPTER SEVEN

A Piece of the Peace

Blessed are the peacemakers: for they shall be called the sons of God.
— *Matthew 5:9*

Of the past 3,400 years, humans have been entirely at peace for 268 of them. That's only 8 percent of recorded history. At least 108 million people were killed in wars in the twentieth century. Estimates for the total number killed in wars throughout all of human history range from 150 million to 1 billion.

According to statistics compiled by Peacemaker Ministries, born-again Christians in the U.S. file as many as 8 million lawsuits every year, often against other Christians, costing as much as 40 billion dollars.

- There are approximately 19,000 major church conflicts in the U.S. each year, an average of 50 per day.

- 32–60% of born-again Christians have gone through a divorce, virtually the same percentage as our general population.
- 1,500 pastors leave their post every month in the U.S., mostly because of conflict.
- Of the 19,000 major conflicts happening in our churches every year, only 2% involve doctrinal issues and 98% involves interpersonal issues. Control issues ranked as the most common cause of conflict, at 85%.
- About 40% of church members who leave their churches do so because of conflict.

Peace: politicians promise it, beauty pageant contestants propagate it, and world leaders promote it. Humanity has searched for this seemingly elusive, precious commodity since Adam and Eve were dragged, kicking and screaming, from the Garden of Eden.

And, according to Thom Rainer, the president and CEO of Lifeway Christian Resources, an entity of the Southern Baptist Convention, 8 out of 10 Southern Baptist churches have either plateaued or are declining and in danger of closing.

Yet, for the most part, the church remains silent about these issues, pushing conflict under the carpet, allowing gossip to spread and looking the other direction.

That is why I am continuously urging our church to pray for *unity*! That is why the word "unity" is capitalized in our church's name, and why our theme verse is "Behold how good and pleasant it is when brethren dwell together in *unity*" (Psalm 133:1).

Why am I so passionate and seemingly obsessed about focusing on unity? Because I have seen firsthand what happens where there is no peace: Ichabod is written on the door to the church, the glory of God departs and we lose our gospel power.

Peace: politicians promise it, beauty pageant contestants propagate it and world leaders promote it. Humanity has searched for this seemingly elusive, precious commodity since Adam and Eve were dragged, kicking and screaming, from the Garden of Eden.

Even the Anti-Christ will use the promise of it to rally the world's politicians, religious leaders and military to his side during the first three-and-a-half years of the Tribulation period.

The politicians have failed, the beauty pageant contestants have come short and the world leaders— well, turn on your TV!

The good news is that even though many—and you may be one of them—have been unable to attain peace, peace has come. "For to us a child is born, to us a son is given; and the government shall be upon his shoulder, and his name shall be called Wonderful Counselor, Mighty God, Everlasting Father, Prince of Peace" (Isaiah 9:6).

The Prince of Peace! Praise God, one day Jesus Christ stepped out from eternity in the midst of chaos, turmoil and war and brought peace to a ravished, dry, parched and weary land.

But knowing that He was about to take on the cross and leave humanity behind, He knew what would happen when His peace departed. He knew:

- Followers would be discouraged.

- Men would be angry and women would cry.

- The out-of-towners would turn their backs to the cross and hit the road home.

- Even His closest disciples would start to doubt and question their beliefs.

Why? Because they all thought peace was gone. So, before He left, He gave some comfort.

"Peace I leave with you; my peace I give to you," said Jesus, "Not as the world gives do I give to you. Let not your hearts be troubled, neither let them be afraid" (John 14:27).

Oh, peace is not gone my friend; it is right here; peace is among us, nay, peace is within us!

That is what makes this next beatitude so powerful and comforting. "Blessed are the peacemakers, for they shall be called the sons of God" (Matthew 5:9).

There are four thoughts I would have us consider as we unpack this verse: *our Christ, our calling, our challenge* and *our celebration*.

Our Christ As the Example of Peace

Let me preface this point by stating how blessed we are to serve a God who never sets us up for failure by calling us to an impossible task. And He never calls us to do that which He was unwilling to do Himself!

Jesus is not found lacking in examples of Him bringing peace to this world! When He entered into this world, He was hailed as the Prince of Peace, and over 2,000 years later, peace can still be found wherever the name of Jesus is uttered!

There are several types of peace that Jesus displayed in practical ways:

- Provisional peace: In Matthew 14, Jesus brought *provisional peace* to the crowd that was hungry and anxious, not knowing where they would get their next meal. Folks out in the middle of nowhere, only having five loaves of bread and two fish for 5,000 people. This large group discovered that, through Jesus Christ, they were able to realize provisional peace; peace in knowing that God takes care of the needs of His children.

- Mental peace: In Mark 5, Jesus brought *mental peace* to the maniac of Gadara, who was possessed with demons, living in a graveyard, torn up in his mind, hailed as crazy by his friends and family and discarded and forgotten by society. This man was able to realize that, through Jesus Christ, mental peace can bring clarity to a troubled, perplexed and anxious mind.

- Practical peace: In John 2, Jesus brought *practical peace* to the host of a wedding who was stressing because the wine had run dry, leaving her feeling overwhelmed and underqualified in life. She was able to realize that, through Jesus Christ, practical peace can overtake the busyness found in everyday life, even when schedules are chaotic, deadlines loom and tasks look unmanageable.

- Emotional peace: In John 4, Jesus brought *emotional peace* to the woman at the well who had a promiscuous past struggling within and was unable to look herself in the mirror because of the sinful life before her. She was able to realize that, through Jesus Christ, no matter where she had been or what she had done, emotional peace can cover every sin like a blanket of grace.

- Physical peace: In John 7, Jesus brought *physical peace* to the woman caught by the religious leaders of the day, the Scribes and Pharisees, who were about to stone her for the sin of adultery. She was able to realize that, through Jesus Christ, no matter what physical calamities may be looming in the future, one can enjoy physical peace through a trust that the future is in the hands of a powerful and loving Savior. And, even if physical healing does not come in this life, it is always guaranteed in the next.

- Spiritual peace: In Mark 16, Jesus brought *spiritual peace* to Peter. Peter, who was so close to Jesus that he was offended at the prospect that he would ever deny his Lord. Yet, there came a day when he did just that. He hurt his testimony, blended into the world and let down those closest to him. Yet, after the resurrection, his Lord appeared on the shore early in the morning and invited Peter to breakfast! Our Lord chose the morning, when the roosters were crowing, to remind Peter of reconciliation through eternal love. Peter realized that, through Jesus Christ, spiritual peace can come in the midst of failure, in finding a Lord who is longsuffering, patient, kind, and forgiving.

When Jesus Christ died, the veil to the Holy of Holies was torn top to bottom and, three days later, the stone was rolled away, revealing an empty tomb from which Jesus Christ emerged in victory, demonstrating once and for all that peace is here to stay!

Now that we have established that Jesus Christ has a history of being the peace-giver, we must acknowledge our calling to be peacemakers, or a piece of the peace, by following His examples of peace.

We must realize that our calling involves:

A Heart of Integrity Filled with Peace

It is great that Jesus brought peace to all of those folks in the Bible when He walked the earth over 2,000 years ago, but greater still that He brings peace to you and me today. Oh, I remember times in my life when I was tossed by circumstance, controlled by emotion and ruled by my sin. I remember times:

- When, like the maniac of Gadara, I was so caught up in my sin and rebellion that I had no *mental peace*. My mind never shut down; I tossed and turned at night, tried to use alcohol, drugs, toxic relationships and money to dull it, but I always came up wanting, until I met Jesus and realized the mental peace that He offers His children.

- When, like the woman at the well, I was so pulled by this world and tossed by circumstance that I had no *emotional peace*. I was driven by emotion and tossed by circumstance with a life marked with defeat, running in survival mode. I was happy when I had money in the bank and sad when there was none. I was smiling when the sun was shining and frowning when it went down. All week I looked forward to the weekend so that I could dull my senses by yielding to temptation and satisfying the flesh, only to start all over again on Monday. That was all before I met Jesus and found that He offers an emotional peace.

And, His peace is constant because it is a peace based on His unchanging love.

- When, like the prostitute before her accusers, I was so afraid of death itself that I had no *physical peace*. I remember in 1987 being in an accident aboard a ship that left me so injured that I had to be airlifted by helicopter from the middle of the Bering Sea. I thought I was going to die. I fell into depression and was flooded with fear and anxiety. That was all before I committed myself to Jesus Christ, who has taken away the very sting of death by turning death into the door that ushers us into the presence of our Great Physician. In fact, for the believer, it is only through death that we can ever experience the physical peace that we long for in this fallen world, where our bodies are in a state of decay.

- When, like the hostess at the wedding, I was feeling so underqualified and overwhelmed for the tasks at hand that I had no *practical peace*. Before Christ I could not even look anyone in the eyes as I had no self-esteem or confidence, buying into the lie that I was worthless and void of anything valuable. Since I became a follower of Christ, while still overwhelmed and underqualified, I have the confidence that whatever task I may face, obstacle I may cross or opponent that may approach, I now know that I can "do all things through Christ who strengthens me" (Philemon 4:13). This is called practical peace.

- When, like the anonymous faces in the crowd, I was so concerned, having more bills than money, that I had no *provisional peace*. I had a habit of staying up late and watching television, especially the "get rich quick" infomercials. In fact, I purchased everything from real estate programs to penny stock investments, all because I was trusting in myself to take care of myself. Now that I have been adopted into the family of God and am His child, I trust Him to provide for my future; this is a provisional peace that only comes from God.

An evangelist friend of mine used to tell the story of how he was on his way to preach a week-long revival. A few states away the engine blew up in his car. The only garage in town gave him the devastating news that since there was no engine within a hundred miles, one had to be ordered. My friend knelt by the hotel room bed and prayed something like, "God, you wanted me to preach a revival two states over. I was on my way, but the engine blew up. So, I am just checking in to let you know that your car is broken and you need to fix it if you want me to preach this revival." Guess what? Within the hour the mechanic called with the unbelievable story of a stranger who came by his shop with a load of automobile parts for sale, among which was an engine that would fit in the evangelist's car! He was on his way the next morning! This is a provisional peace that is only offered through Jesus Christ.

- When, like Peter, the many times that I had let my Lord down, hurt those closest to me and felt lonely, rejected and tossed aside, even by God Himself, I had no spiritual peace. It hurts too much to think of all of the times that I have let my Lord down by my disobedience and sin, yet to know that He will never throw in the towel, wipe His hands, turn His back and walk away from me gives me a spiritual peace that only comes from a relationship with Him.

Only Jesus can offer something this world knows nothing about: peace. As Jesus Christ came to a dry and thirsty land to bring peace, He has come to our dry and thirsty hearts.

Once we have internal peace, we must focus on the external. You cannot bring peace to others until you have experienced a peace from within.

This is our calling: we must stand in the midst of humanity and evaluate the culture honestly—even though many people are going around like the prophet Jeremiah, declaring peace when there is no peace.

Even Paul warns, "While people are saying, 'There is peace and security,' then sudden destruction will come upon them as labor pains come upon a pregnant woman, and they will not escape" (1 Thessalonians 5:3).

As children of God, we must not be fooled by a world that declares peace. We must always be honest in our evaluation, recognizing there are many around us who do not enjoy the peace that is residing in us. Understanding that peace can only come from Christ, not from legislation, prohibition, institution, extrinsic motivation or intestinal fortitude. Peace comes only from Christ and Christ alone.

An example of this falsely perceived peace is evident when someone dies, especially in Hollywood, in that everyone is quick to put R.I.P. on the gravestone or write it in the paper, post it on social media and even proclaim it from the pulpit.

But we know the truth: there is no rest in peace in the next life until you claim the Prince of Peace in this life, Jesus Christ.

When we become a piece of the peace as Jesus was, we experience:

An Increased Risk for Attempting Peace

If you are the kind of Christian who runs from conflict, buries your head in the sand, simply prays for dissension and tolerates disunity, then please hear the words of Jesus in Matthew 10:35–39:

"For I have come to set a man against his father, and a daughter against her mother, and a daughter-in-law against her mother-in-law. And a person's enemies will be those of his own household. Whoever loves father or mother more than me is not worthy of me, and whoever loves son or daughter more than me is not worthy of me. And whoever does not take his cross and follow me is not worthy of me. Whoever finds his life will lose it, and whoever loses his life for my sake will find it."

What does all of this mean? It means that when you are a piece of the peace, the peacemaker God has called and empowered you to be, you will be in the very presence of *conflict*.

In fact, you might even *be* that conflict. Christians are dropping out of church, members are fussing and fighting, churches are splitting, ministries are closing, pastors are quitting and souls are dying to a devil's hell every single day. We have work to do and peace to bring. That is our calling.

Our Challenge to Show That Example of Peace

Your challenge is simple: be who God has called you to be, in:

Disposition

The first thing Jesus tells us to be, once we have the truths of the beatitudes in us, is the salt and the light! Oh, the peace that would come into this world if Christians would simply let His light shine before men!

Are you walking around defeated? With your head hung low? You are not being a piece of the peace if country singers are following you around for inspiration or if you look like you've been baptized in pickle juice and sucking on a lemon. You can't be a piece of the peace if you are going through life with your arms crossed, lips out, with "Bless me if you can" on your swollen tongue. I remember a Christian comedian shouting to a group in church something like, "Don't make me send a missionary to your face!"

> *Radical lifestyle evangelism is a salve from Satan that is applied to the lazy, complacent Christian to soothe the guilt that comes from not being faithful to the Great Commission.*

Friend, this world has its fair share of defeated, miserable and broken people. It's time to show them transformed and renewed lives that shout joy, hope, love, power and victory! Being a piece of the peace means that because we have been filled with peace from God, we have lives that reflect God. It means going through this life with our chest out, chin up, a smile on our face and a spring in our step because there is joy in our heart! We must have a peaceful disposition. And, we must have peaceful:

Conversation

Our mission is to spread the gospel and make disciples; to reproduce and create other peacemakers. It is way overdue for us to step forward, reach outward and speak upward. I dislike the trite saying applied to evangelism, "Spread the gospel and use words if necessary." This is like saying, "Go feed the hungry and use food if necessary." This is my issue with radical lifestyle evangelism: the idea that somehow, just by the lives we live, the lost will be drawn to us like a magnet and transformed by the power of the gospel, without us saying a word!

In my opinion, radical lifestyle evangelism is a salve from Satan that is applied to the lazy, complacent Christian to soothe the guilt that comes from not being faithful to the Great Commission. We must not be ashamed of the gospel of Christ. While the lives we live must back up the words we give, we must "preach the word," being ready "in season and out of season" to "reprove, rebuke, and exhort, with complete patience and teaching" (2 Timothy 4:2). This beatitude does not say to be peaceful, which is what we enjoy internally; it says to be a peace*maker*, which is what we do externally: we make peace.

And, being a piece of the peace requires:

Navigation

We must be proactive. So many believers turn away when there is conflict, shirking their responsibility. This is mostly due to fear. Too many Christians have come to believe the loud voices of the godless minority in this country proclaiming that they are the true majority. The result is that Christians have been silenced and the church has lost its power. We have been called and empowered to rise up, speak out and be a piece of the peace. To act on the belief that "greater is He that is in you than he that is in this world" (1 John 4:4).

Years ago in a church service, the choir director had everyone seated through a congregational song. This is not unheard of, but the song happened to be "Stand Up, Stand Up for Jesus!" This is what is going on in our world as believers refuse to be the peacemakers God has called them to be while they navigate through this life.

Our Celebration for Being That Example of Peace

The reward for being a piece of the peace? We are called sons of God. This is a title that will usher us into His presence. A title that has changed my very life down here and will provide new life up there. What does this title mean? Well, it means several things, actually; the first speaks of:

Nativity Sonship

The very fact that Jesus Christ was born of a virgin means that He was, is, and forever will be known not as "Jesus Christ, son of Joseph" but as "Jesus Christ, Son of God"!

And this means that Father God is now our Father through Christ. You might not have been able to find a great dad on this earth, but you will find no better Father than the One offered in God through His Son Jesus Christ.

And, this speaks of:

Covenant Sonship

This focuses on the fact that Jesus Christ lived a sinless life before His Father God and His creation, so that He was able to have a relationship with God that was never severed due to sin.

Because of this, He now offers us to share in this covenant sonship with God the Father *through* Him. When we stand before a Holy and Almighty God, He no longer sees our sin, but His Son, our Savior. So stop trying to forgive yourself and start enjoying the forgiveness that He has already provided through covenant sonship.

This also speaks of:

Messianic Sonship

At the cross Jesus cried out: "It is finished!" — meaning He had defeated sin, Satan and even death. And, that He started building His kingdom and will be returning soon!

This world might think it has the upper hand by removing prayer from school, tossing aside the Ten Commandments and boldly demanding a separation of church and state, as they celebrate sin and spread their wicked agenda through godless organizations like the American Civil Liberty Union and the Freedom from Religion Foundation, celebrating one legal victory after another.

The devil himself seems to have gotten quite smug and comfortable on this earth, acting like a mouse at play while the cat is away.

Let it be known that Jesus is coming back, not as a lamb led to the slaughter, but as the Lion of the tribe of Judah.

He will come in full pomp and power. Revelation 19:11–16 says, "Heaven opened, and behold, a white horse. And He who sat on him was called Faithful and True, and in righteousness He judges and makes war. His eyes were like a flame of fire, and on His head were many crowns. He had a name written that no one knew except Himself. He was clothed with a robe dipped in blood, and His name is called The Word of God. And the armies in heaven, clothed in fine linen, white and clean, followed Him on white horses. Now out of His mouth goes a sharp sword, that with it He should strike the nations. And He Himself will rule them with a rod of iron. He Himself treads the winepress of the fierceness and wrath of Almighty God. And He has on His robe and on His thigh a name written: King of Kings and Lord of Lords."

And since we are sons of God, we will be right behind Him. In fact, we will have a front row seat to watch Satan, the Anti-Christ and the false prophet cast into the lake of fire as we celebrate the end of sin, collectively singing "Victory in Jesus!" for all eternity! That is what Messianic sonship is all about.

Lastly, this title speaks of:

Personal Sonship

Jesus Christ has a personal and intimate relationship with Father God and—as sons of God—so do we! Never take that for granted. As sons of God, we have audience with the Lord of lords and the King of kings. He actually hears, cares and is able to move on our behalf. He loves us.

When CommUNITY Church grew to the point that we started using bulletins, I had four Bible verses printed on the bottom of each one, and there to this day they remain: "The sun stood still" (Joshua 10:13); "The iron did swim" (2 Kings 6:6); "This God is our God" (Psalm 48:14); and "Rejoice in the Lord always" (Philippians 4:4).

I have held many titles through the years: Son, Petty Officer, Husband, Father, Coach, Professor, and Pastor, to name a few. Each of these titles conveys some type of authority, position and description. Some were earned, others were thrust upon me, but all are from this world. But there is a title that trumps all of these, and that title is Son of God. This is a title that was unearned yet is more cherished than any other, for it is not earthly in origin but heavenly, not temporal but eternal. I was asked a few weeks ago what I would want stated on my gravestone; I did not have to think on that too long! Oh, how much it would communicate for my tombstone to simply read "Tom McCracken—Son of God"!

There are benefits to being called sons of God. But there is only one way that you can be called a son of God, and it's by being a peacemaker.

There is peace available in this world; the question is: will you be a piece of the peace?

Blessed are the peacemakers: for they shall be called the sons of God.
— **Matthew 5:9**

CHAPTER EIGHT

Steps to Victory

Before we move on and unpack the last of the beatitudes, and discover our ultimate reward, let's review to keep it all in context.

One of the problems facing our culture is that we like to have the best now. We are a self-entitled and instant society. We shun work. We are lazy. We expect to have everything our grandparents had without going through the sweat, blood, time and work to have it.

This attitude has crept into the church in the past few years, and so many think that they should have "Peter walking on water" faith the moment they become Christians.

That is why the *health and wealth prosperity* message of today is taking root in our churches. Its message can be summed up by: greatness now! This is verified by the title of a book written by a leader in the prosperity camp, *Your Best Life Now. [11]*

Listen, Christianity is tough. It is hard. It is a journey. It is not instant. Like John MacArthur once said, "If this is your best life now, you are on your way to hell!" [12]

Ever see someone demonstrate great faith through difficult times? I have. In fact, one of the greatest displays of faith that Christ was enough in a life came from a lady in a nursing home. We will call her Gloria. I had heard through our membership about Gloria, who had been in a terrible car accident in which she lost everything. So, I decided that I would go out to that nursing home and visit with Gloria to encourage her heart and pray for her.

When I entered the room, I found a bright-eyed owner of one of those "light up a room" smiles! Certainly I had the wrong room. Nope. After a few minutes I found out that in one tragic car accident she had lost her husband, her legs, her dog, her car and even her house, as the sale money was used to pay for her medical bills. Almost in tears after hearing this story, I asked if I could pray for her, to which she replied something like, "I am fine! I still have my Jesus, and He is enough. Let's pray together for all of the hurting and lonely folks in this nursing home." Wow! But, that is not the kicker! After I left that room, I went to the nurse's station to ask how long she would be at the facility and to make my intentions of future visits known. Get this: the nurse told me to check at the information desk before each visit because she was never in the same room. Do you know why? The nursing staff was moving her from room to room to encourage other patients who were discouraged from knee and hip surgeries!

You do not get that kind of faith instantly or without work. That is why I love the beatitudes. It is here we discover the Christian journey presented in eight steps—eight steps that lead to a victorious, meaningful life; a life full of power, for it is a life full of purpose.

Take a step, receive a reward and move up. Take another, receive a reward, and move up. And by the time you hit the eighth rung of this ladder, you claim victory!

In fact, these beatitudes have such a progression that when you reach the eighth rung, it is as if you have fought in the Roman coliseum, won the battle and made your way up the stairs to the Emperor, and are prepared to be awarded a crown of victory—your ultimate reward!

As I stated earlier, these eight steps should be divided into two segments: the first four steps deal with our relationship with God, and the last four deals with our relationships with each other.

Our Relationship with God

Step One: Poverty

Blessed are the poor in spirit for theirs is the kingdom of heaven.
— Matthew 5:3

This does not mean that God blesses those who have no value. Everybody is somebody! For you are created in the image and likeness of God. "The Lord your God is in your midst, a mighty one who will save; he will rejoice over you with gladness; he will quiet you by his love; he will exult over you with loud singing" (Zephaniah 3:17).

Do not believe the devil's lie that you have no value. You are a creation of the living God, and He loves you with an everlasting love.

To be poor in spirit is to understand that there is nothing you can do to elevate yourself and claim heaven as your future home.

There are no celestial scales that will weigh your good works against your bad ones and *if* the scales tip in your favor, God will allow you entrance into heaven. Those scales simply do not exist.

You can't bring your Bible study, church attendance, money, good deeds, intelligence, baptism, church membership, degrees or positions held as tickets for admittance into heaven.

So, if we can't be *good enough* to reach heaven, how then are we to obtain a confidence that heaven is our future home?

If God believed that your need was so great that He had to sacrifice His only Son, you must believe that your need is great enough to necessitate that kind of sacrifice.

Rick Warren shook a selfish culture in his book *The Purpose Driven Life* with the revelation that, on earth, it is not about us *[13]*. Guess what? In heaven it is not about us, either!

Friend, only a humble cry of brokenness will move God's hand of grace in your direction. It is not about what you do or who you are, but what He has done and who He is.

One day God looked down at a sinful humanity marked with rebellion and pride and said to His only begotten Son, Jesus Christ, *I want you to leave glory, don the robes of humanity, be born of a virgin, and become one of them in order to save all of them. Live, laugh and love for 33 years, then lay your life down. Suffer; be rejected, despised and hang on the cross made from the tree that you planted thousands of years ago, suspended halfway between your home and halfway between your world, with both worlds turning their backs on you as you are left to die. On the third day, you will have the power and authority to raise yourself from the dead, defeating sin, Satan and even death itself! You will walk out of that borrowed tomb demonstrating to an unbelieving world that they can't keep a good Man down!*

If God believed that your need was so great that He had to sacrifice His only Son, you must believe that your need is great enough to necessitate that kind of sacrifice.

You will never enjoy a saving relationship with God until you *need* a saving relationship with God. And when you cry out with that poor spirit, He will give you the kingdom of heaven. Now that is a reward!

To be taken from the grips of sin and placed in the grips of His grace. To change your father from Satan to Savior. From being controlled by sin to being guided by the Spirit. From hell to heaven, Sinai to Zion, wretched to wealthy, fear to faith, death to life, darkness to light, from "woe is me" to "been set free." That is our reward through salvation!

Step Two: Mourning

Blessed are those who mourn for they shall be comforted.
— *Matthew 5:4*

Recently, in one of the small group sessions in our church, a teacher asked the class, "What do the world and the church share in common?" The class was silent, so he then answered for them, "We are all sinners!" Why was the class silent? Because to understand the "why" of the cross makes us uncomfortable because it forces us to admit that we were the ones who caused Jesus Christ to die on the cross.

And, while our *goodness* can never reach high enough, His *grace* can reach low enough.

It always causes me to chuckle whenever I hear someone declare, "I found God," because I know that God was never lost! We are the ones who were lost in the ocean of our sin, and the only way He can find you bobbing around in that ocean is for you to send up the Matthew 5:3 beacon by confessing you are spiritually bankrupt, in need of rescue.

Once you've repented of your sins, you are adopted by the King of kings and Lord of lords; you are now a child of God, and your life has been touched by the love of the Master's hand.

You now have the best Father a child could ever hope for or dream of. And, because of this, you want to show Him that you are thankful that He saved you, changed you and set you free.

The great news with our Father is that you don't have to *prove* to Him that you love Him by your works, but through your works you seek to *please* Him as proof of your love for Him.

And we do that by mourning, weeping and grieving over our sin *and* the sins of those around us. Why? Because we know that sin hurts our Father. And for those who have taken that first step, what hurts Him hurts us. We know sin is what caused our Savior to suffer, bleed and die, and we don't want to put Him through that ever again. Sin hurts the very heart of the only One who has loved us with an everlasting love.

And what is our reward for caring about our sin so much that we mourn over it? He rewards us with comfort! In sin we carry around baggage, separation, scars, fear, guilt, shame and doubt. Yet Jesus Christ tells us that when we mourn over that very sin, He will comfort us.

Step Three: Meekness

Blessed are the meek, for they shall inherit the earth.
— *Matthew 5:5*

Praise God that when we surrender to the cross, He gives us a power to leave the devil, break free from sin, crucify the flesh, overcome the world and have hope, joy, love and the power to walk through this sinful, hurtful, wicked world full of trials, troubles and tribulation—with a smile on our face, spring in our step, joy in our heart and victory in life.

Now, what do we do with this power in us? We demonstrate meekness. As Kenny Rogers would say, "You got to know when to hold 'em, know when to fold 'em, know when to walk away, and know when to run!" [14]

As a child of God, there are times we need to use the power within us to control that power within us. When it comes to our feelings, emotions, pride, preferences, visions, dreams and goals, we should turn the other cheek, let go and let God.

Ever watch the television show *Reba*? In one episode Reba was stressing about something and Van said, "I've got one word for you, let it go!" To which Reba replied, "Van, that is three words." Van said, "Not the way I say it, letitgo!" [15]

You can apply that same concept to walking the Christian walk:

- Church is not going where you want on a mission trip? Let it go!

- Pastor didn't shake your hand on Sunday? Let it go!

- Carpet not your color? Let it go!

- Prefer pews over chairs? Let it go!

- Suits instead of jeans? Let it go!

- Contemporary music over a traditional hymnal? Let it go!

- Want the preaching to last only 20 minutes? Let it go!

While there are times to "let it go," or be gentle, there are also times to be a giant as there are things worth fighting for:

- The helpless widow who is being taken advantage of.

- The lonely husband in the waiting room.

- The abandoned child in the orphanage.

- The special-needs person who is being mocked.

- The doctrines of His Word.

- The unity within His church.

The key is to know when to be gentle and when to be a giant, or using the power to *control* the power.

So, what rewards do you get when you take this step and demonstrate meekness? We inherit the earth, both now and then. Or, simply put, power in this life and peace in the next.

Step Four: Hungering and Thirsting

Blessed are those who hunger and thirst for righteousness, for they shall be satisfied.
— ***Matthew 5:6***

Jesus wants His children to get to the point where we have a deep, insatiable, continuous craving for righteousness.

There was a time when I hungered and thirsted after the things of this world—power, popularity, possessions, promotions and prestige—and I was never satisfied; I had a void in my life.

Remember, God created that void. He placed an eternity in our hearts; it is woven into our DNA!

After taking these steps, I can tell you now, with no hesitation, Jesus is enough. I have been made new by the love of God, and now I live each day in awe. I have never gotten over the wonder of it all. I'm completely satisfied with Jesus.

That is why I can be found:

- In church on Sundays and Wednesdays, learning more *about* Him.

- In the hospitals, nursing homes and funeral homes, telling others *of* Him.

- At church workdays, on the mission field and in the neighborhoods, serving with others *for* Him.

- At fellowships, banquets, picnics and gatherings, enjoying others who *love* Him.

I can't get enough of Him. And the reward for that? Satisfaction. We can all enjoy what it means to be full of power in this life and have peace in the next because of a life full of purpose and meaning. That is what Jesus is offering.

Well, that brings us to the end of the first four beatitudes, those that deal with our relationship with God.

In review: while you walked up these steps, submitting to God, while unworthy and undeserving, you were rewarded with the kingdom of heaven, comfort, the earth and satisfaction.

These next steps tell you what to do with all that you have been given. In other words, letting out what has been let in!

The tragic reality is that most "Christians" stop after the first four beatitudes, the *getting* part, and they never move on to the last four, the *giving* part.

And, folks think that they can be right with God but have issues with people. You can't separate your love for God and your love for people; these are married concepts that go hand in hand. In order to be *right* with God, you must be *right* with people! The Apostle John puts it like this: "If anyone says, 'I love God,' and hates his brother, he is a liar; for the one who does not love his brother whom he has seen, cannot love God whom he has not seen" (1 John 4:20).

So, how do we make sure that we love others? By taking the next steps.

Our Relationships with Each Other

Step Five: Compassion

Blessed are the merciful, for they shall receive mercy.
— *Matthew 5:7*

I have stated that I like to view the beatitudes as the ladder that takes us up and closer to God, ultimately bringing us into a victorious Christian life. So, each step follows the previous one, building on each other. This is very evident with this step as we transition from our relationship with God to our relationships with each other.

So, what does mercy mean? What does a life that is compassionate look like? Well, once I realize that I am poor in spirit, I understand there is nothing within me that is righteous, so as a worm I cry out in my lost condition for rescue. And the One who comes to my rescue is a Father who knows me better than everyone else does, yet chooses to love me more than anyone else does.

So I mourn over my sin and the sins of others because I know that sin hurts the very One who loved me enough to rescue me. And, because I know how undeserving I am, I know that I am not better than anyone, just better off. My position in God, through Christ, is tempered with meekness. For I am who I am only by His grace. I know that if anyone knew the real me—where I have been, what I have done, what goes through my mind—I would be alone in this world.

So, because I know me as I do and that God loves me anyway, meekness marks my very life. And because God came through the door of my life when everyone else was running out, I have a hungering and thirsting for Him. Why wouldn't I? He is the only one who gave His life so that I could know what living really is!

So, does it not make sense that once I have enjoyed all of the benefits of the love of God, I should view my fellow man in a different light? Through the eyes of grace and the lenses of His love? That is what being merciful means: to have compassion on other sinners! To look at those outside of His grace with pity and sorrow, knowing they are being held captive by Satan and can't help themselves. This mercy becomes compassion in action as we reach out with His love to rescue the perishing!

Step Six: Purity

> *Blessed are those that are pure in heart, for they shall see God.*
> — *Matthew 5:8*

Purity means getting to the point in your life where you have achieved complete clarity and focus on the things of God by banishing evil from your life, to enjoy the freedoms in Christ that He longs for you to have.

It is simply being honest before God in your evaluation of who you are and who He is, and then allowing God to be God in and through your life.

> *It's bad enough that folks don't love each other in the church, but even more tragic is that this lost world, in desperate need of peace, is looking to the church for answers and walking away empty.*

While purity affects your relationship with God, your purity also has an impact on this world. This world is watching you. Your life is a stage. And, they will not be fooled by the Bible carrying, Christian radio playing, Christian flag waving, "Property of God" T-shirt wearing, fish magnet displaying, fair-weather Christian who has become the majority in American church culture.

This world is *not* watching you when everything is going well in your life; they only tune in when life gets tough, when things go south. For they want to see if what you are wearing, watching, waving, playing and displaying is the real deal; they want to know if you're pure in heart. So, we must show them, like Gloria in the nursing home, that while we are not perfect, we are pure.

The reward for reaching this step and achieving purity in heart? Seeing God! Seeing God means that we are able to:

- Bless those who curse us, because we see that pleasing God is our only goal.

- Go through times of severe trials and suffering because we see that God is able to work all things together for those who love Him.

- Reach out to the unreachable and love the unlovable because we see that we can do all things through Christ who gives us strength.

- Cast all of our cares and burdens upon Him because we see that God cares for us.

- Not worry about tomorrow because we see that God holds tomorrow in His hand.

So, the reward for being pure in heart is to see God change lives *around you* because of the love displayed *through you* by the grace provided *to you*.

Step Seven: Peacemaking

Blessed are the peacemakers, for they shall be called the sons of God.
— *Matthew 5:9*

This culture longs for peace. This world is tired and weary of conflict. They see it between husband and wife, parent and child, employers and employees, brothers and sisters, Republicans and Democrats, and nations against nations.

The church should be the example of peace instead of these statistics:

- 3,500 people leaving the church every day

- 7,000 churches closing every year

- 70% of those between the ages of 18 and 22 dropping out of church

It's bad enough that folks don't love each other in the church, but even more tragic is that this lost world, in desperate need of peace, is looking to the church for answers and walking away empty.

They look within and see the same conflict they see at home, in politics, at work, on TV, in clubs and in other organizations.

And since they walk away not seeing a difference, they walk away unchanged. We are missing the mark.

1 Thessalonians 5:14–15 says, "We urge you, brethren, admonish the unruly, encourage the fainthearted, help the weak, be patient with everyone. See that no one repays another with evil for evil, but always seek after that which is good for one another and for all people."

D. L. Moody had it right when he declared, "The preaching that this world needs most is the sermons in shoes that are walking with Jesus Christ."

Now that you have completed all seven steps, the eighth step awaits, which is where you find out what reward you get for *Being the Believing*!

CHAPTER NINE

It Hurts So Good

Blessed are those who are persecuted for righteousness'
sake, for theirs is the kingdom of heaven.
— *Matthew 5:10*

Imagine in your youth reading of a promised Messiah who would one day come to set the captives free, establish His kingdom, banish the wicked and rule with a rod of iron through love and power.

A Messiah who would bring salvation to the lost, comfort to the mourning and restoration of the land to the meek; give satisfaction to the longing and mercy to the merciful; reveal Himself to the pure in heart; and adopt and title those who would strive for peace.

Now, here you are as an adult, sitting at the base of a mountain in the middle of nowhere, looking at this man who claims to be that very Messiah, listening to Him preach, hanging on His every word, hoping beyond hope that now is the time and today is that day.

And He says, "Blessed are the poor in spirit, for theirs is the kingdom of heaven. Blessed are those who mourn, for they shall be comforted. Blessed are the meek, for they shall inherit the earth. Blessed are those who hunger and thirst for righteousness, for they shall be satisfied. Blessed are the merciful, for they shall receive mercy. Blessed are the pure in heart, for they shall see God. Blessed are the peacemakers, for they shall be called sons of God."

Imagine your excitement sitting at the base of that mountain as Jesus Christ, the Messiah, preaches through the greatest sermon ever preached, promising great rewards for, and the demonstration of, that faith.

Imagine being in that audience—weary and tired of being ruled over, taken advantage of and mistreated, not to mention being viewed as a stranger in your own Promised Land.

Imagine what these words would mean. Life-changing. Rewarding. And as if these first seven rewards were not grand enough, He was saving the best for last, as all great teachers do. Starting off slow but then building up the momentum, creating an anticipation that intensifies, stimulating an emotional eruption.

So, there you are, on cloud nine, excited about this last reward like a child who saved the biggest gift under the tree for last. Then Jesus unpacks the last gift in verse 10 by saying, "Blessed are those who are persecuted for righteousness' sake, for theirs is the kingdom of heaven."

You would be shocked! And, so was this crowd! They were expecting that by the time they admitted they were poor, wept over their sin, displayed meekness, hungered and thirsted after the things of God, showed compassion, shunned hypocrisy and brought peace to the world, they would be getting knighted!

But, do all these things and Jesus says your reward is persecution? Heck, you send in $100 to a television evangelist and even he promises you prosperity and puts your name on the TV screen for the whole world to see.

The truth is that if you are not being persecuted, you are not Being the Believing!

Jesus knew that this crowd was shocked. How do I know that? Well, for seven beatitudes, Jesus spoke in the third person, using words like "they," "theirs" and "those"; yet after He reveals that the ultimate reward for Being the Believing is persecution, He settles His eternally loving eyes on the crowd and brings an explanation, as well as personalization with a simple word: "you." If you are not careful, you will miss that subtle shift from third person to second person.

After He knows they are struggling with the idea of persecution, Jesus says, "Blessed are *you*." He makes it personal and then brings an explanation.

Here are two reasons why:

- First, to reveal that true Christianity is tough, which naturally ushers in an element of anxiety.

So, Jesus is revealing that while persecution will come to the Christian, there is a divine purpose; while the first seven beatitudes are about *character*, this last one is about *confirmation*. When we go to the doctor and have to receive a shot, it is helpful for us to know that the shot is needed and serves a bigger purpose. So, Jesus looks into the eyes of those struggling with the prospect that persecution will come and provides *confirmation* that persecution has a purpose.

- And second, to bring *comfort* to those who may be scared, thrown off, anxious, and discouraged that the expectation in Christianity is to be persecuted. How like our Father, not only to educate His patients that while the shot will hurt, it has a purpose, but also to make it personal by looking lovingly into the eyes of those patients and, reminding them that in addition to being the Great Physician, He will be with them through it all.

In our text we find that the very proof in the pudding for Being the Believing is whether or not you are being persecuted. And for the most part, Christians in America are not being persecuted. So, either God had it wrong and should have exempted America from this text, or we as Christians in America have it wrong because we are not living the way Jesus said we are to live.

The truth is that if you are not being persecuted, you are not Being the Believing!

Why did Jesus save this beatitude for last? In the words of Kent Hughes: "Its position at the end of the list tells us that it is of supreme importance to the church. Significantly, when stretched on the loom of adversity the church has repeatedly woven persecution and joy into garments of divine praise."

I would add that another reason Jesus saved this for last was to weed out the players, the fence riders, the non-committal and the lukewarm.

Anyone who would step up into Christianity after hearing that they would possibly lose their families, homes, jobs, property and very lives is someone who can change this world.

Reviled Because of Your Faith

Blessed are those who are persecuted for righteousness' sake, for theirs is the kingdom of heaven.
— *Matthew 5:10*

Jesus establishes from the get-go that the reason Christians will be persecuted is not because of their personality, bad decisions, past or sin, but because of the Savior. This kind of persecution is motivated by two thoughts:

For Righteousness' Sake

1 Peter 4:3–4 says, "For the time that is past suffices for doing what the Gentiles want to do, living in sensuality, passions, drunkenness, orgies, drinking parties, and lawless idolatry. With respect to this they are surprised when you do not join them in the same flood of debauchery, and they malign you."

Like many of you, I had my time with this world and all of its pleasures, and after tasting all of what the world had to offer, I was still not satisfied. I still had a void within me, and I still had no peace. I always walked away from the things of this world empty, wanting and unsatisfied.

Then I met Jesus, and by His grace, I can boldly declare that I have tasted my Lord and found Him to be good, to be enough. I am satisfied.

The time of doing what this world wants is over, and when they hear that I am finished, they do not understand and they bring persecution.

This world has always persecuted what it does not understand. So, be peculiar, unique and different, and when—not if, but when—persecution comes, rejoice because you know that persecution means you are doing it right!

For Christ's Account

Persecution has always come to those who have associated with Christ. It's called persecution through proximity. That is why Peter distanced himself from our Lord and hung out with the heathen instead.

He was trying to prove that he was not a disciple of Jesus so he could escape the persecution that comes from associating with Jesus.

If you do not want to be persecuted, become one with the world. And, if it's any comfort, you will be in the majority, whether you're at home, in the office or even at church.

But, if you are one of the few who long for the day when you can stand before our Father and hear those eternally comforting words, "Well done, good and faithful servant. You have been faithful over a little; I will set you over much. Enter into the joy of your master" (Matthew 25:23), then you will welcome persecution because it is by that very persecution that your life is confirmed, approved, or blessed by God.

A Reaction to Your Faith

Blessed are you when others revile you and persecute you and utter all kinds of evil against you falsely on my account.
— Matthew 5:11

Why will we be persecuted? Because of everything we stand for and all that we believe. Our Founder, whom we love, follow and serve, is the only good in this world. Why does this world hate us to the degree that they cause us to suffer when we are all about goodness?

You will suffer because you are called out! "If ye were of the world, the world would love his own: but because ye are not of the world, but I have chosen you out of the world, therefore the world hateth you" (John 15:19).

Talk about being upfront. If you are a true believer and possess the seven beatitudes, you will receive persecution. In a culture where most have traded persecution for pleasure purposely, this is a shocking concept.

I remember standing outside the front doors of the church after a Sunday service, greeting people, when an older gentleman grabbed my hand and asked with a smile, "How has the world been treating you?"—to which I replied, "The world hates me!" You should have seen the way this man looked at me. He looked at me like a cow looks at a new gate: perplexed. Next thing I know, he is going to the deacons, requesting prayer for me as he thought I was depressed from a bad week!

If you are living for Jesus, expect suffering. Jesus made this fact very clear, for He said, "If the world hates you, you know that it has hated Me before it hated you" (John 15:18).

You will suffer because you will remove the cloak of sin. "Yea, and all that will live *godly* in Christ Jesus *shall* suffer persecution" (2 Timothy 3:12).

The true believer should live in such a way that, when beside an unbeliever or the backslidden Christian, they expose their sin. Folks will either get right, get going or get attacking.

While this is a foreign concept to American Christianity, it was not new to the early church. Next to the unbeliever, the Christian used to stick out like a sore thumb! And, again, people persecute that which they do not understand. So, when you refuse to compromise and conform to this world by what you do, where you go, what you watch and what you wear because of who you love, suffering will mark your life because you have removed the cloak of sin worn by those around you.

You will suffer because this world does not know Christ. "And these things will they do unto you, because they have not known the Father, nor me" (John 16:3).

There are many "religious" people in this world. In fact, according to statistics, as many as 98% of the world's population believes in something greater than themselves.

In fact, if you consider the major religions of the world—Christianity, Islam, Hinduism, Buddhism, Shinto, Sikhism, Judaism, Confucianism, Taoism/Daoism and Jainism—you will find almost 7 billion adherents to a religion. Amazingly, the world's population in 2013 was only 7.125 billion!

Additionally, if you count the indigenous religions, you will soon discover that the true atheists are really the true minority. And yet, even with all of these people claiming to believe in something, we are still living in a world full of sin. People are defeated and hopeless, and have no peace.

Why? Because while this world may know a religion, this world does not know Christ. Years ago in North Carolina, I drove by a church sign that read, "Know God, know peace. No God, no peace." That says it all, for peace only comes from the One born in a manger over 2,000 years ago, who was introduced to humanity in Isaiah 9:6 as the "Wonderful Counselor, Mighty God, Everlasting Father, Prince of *Peace*."

It is not the Muslim, Hindu, Buddhist, Shinto, Sikh, Jewish, Confucian, Taoist, Daoist or Jain way. When Jesus stepped out from eternity and introduced Himself to humanity, He boldly declared, "I am the way, the truth and the life, no man comes to the Father but by me" (John 14:6). And, by that statement alone, He offends every tribe, tongue, kindred, nation and people group that claims there are other ways to heaven.

Stand on the rooftops and shout from the highways that Jesus Christ is the only way to salvation, and you will suffer because this world does not know Christ and they will reject any god other than one they can create and manipulate.

You want to see persecution? Tell the 1.8 billion Muslims who worship Allah that they are on the path to hell.

Tell the 1.1 billion Hindus, who worship over 330 million gods and goddesses, that their worship is in vain.

Tell the Buddhists that their founder, Siddhartha, was deceived by a demon and their prayers are not being heard.

Tell the nation of China and the nation of Japan that Confucianism and Shinto will not lead to Moksha or Nirvana.

Stand on the rooftops and shout from the highways that Jesus Christ is the only way to salvation, and you will suffer because this world does not know Christ and they will *reject* any god outside of the one they can create and manipulate. In contrast, they will *receive* any god that will not judge their sin or seek to change how they live and who they want to be.

You will suffer because this world is deceived in its concept of God! John 16:1–4 says, "These things have I spoken unto you, that ye should not be offended. They shall put you out of the synagogues: yea, the time cometh, that whosoever killeth you will think that he doeth God service. And these things will they do unto you, because they have not known the Father, nor me. But these things have I told you, that when the time shall come, ye may remember that I told you of them. And these things I said not unto you at the beginning, because I was with you."

> *If you are Being the Believing, you will suffer because this world is deceived in its concept of God.*

If you are Being the Believing, you will suffer because this world is deceived in its concept of God.

This world will take no issue with certain attributes of God or segments of the Bible. In fact, most love to hear that God is an ever-present help in time of trouble and that He will protect, provide for, give strength to, and unconditionally love all people.

Their perverted view is that God has created a world of roses and we are all His children, holding hands and singing "Kumbaya" as we enjoy His love all the way to heaven.

But things get ugly and persecution comes when you start to talk about His holiness, wrath, anger, hatred of sin, accountability and His call to repentance.

I love how J. Vernon McGee responded to this issue. When someone wrote him a letter, they likened heaven unto the post office in their small town. In effect, they pointed out that they could get to this post office by taking a dirt road, the highway, by means of a short cut or by using the new paved road. So, they figured, with all of the different religions out there, that heaven must be the same way: many roads all leading to one place. McGee simply replied, "The problem with this thinking is that when we die we do not go to the Post Office!"

Our Suffering Is for a Purpose

Suffering for Christ brings us closer *to* Him, makes us more *like* Him and reminds us that we are *of* Him. Luther once said, "I am getting rather proud, for I see that my character is more and more defamed."

> *This present existence has a very short shelf-life!*

As of this writing, I am running for a seat on the local school board. Someone wrote an editorial and submitted it to the local paper in support of my campaign. One of the deacons of our church viewed some of the comments on that editorial and was concerned that I would be upset by some of the negative remarks against me, which ranged from calling me a "religious nut" to likening me to a member of ISIS!

But, I was far from upset. In fact, I rejoiced! Why? Because when we are Being the Believing and doing Christianity right, we will suffer persecution and can be confident that this suffering has a purpose.

Our Suffering Is Not Permanent

There is coming a day when those clouds will be rolled back like a scroll, the trump shall resound and our Lord shall descend.

A day when my Jesus will show all of those faith healers how it's really done by whisking the Holy Spirit down every hallway of every nursing home and hospital, past every room where born-again believers are hurting and lonely, longing for relief and peace, and He will give them a new body that will have no need for medications, visitations or lamentations. This present existence has a very short shelf-life!

When my oldest daughter, who is in the United States Air Force, was at technical school in Texas for three months, she discovered she was the only virgin in her flight. She was the only one who went to church every Sunday and the only one who said "no" when literally everyone else around her enjoyed the things of the world. As a result, there were times that she felt lonely and became tired of being isolated, often being alone on the weekends.

For those like my daughter, living for Christ and facing the promised persecution, there is comfort in the knowledge that our suffering is not permanent. For there is coming a day, and it will be soon, when we will either come into His presence through the casket or the clouds and will realize when we trade in our faith for sight at the Gates of Glory and look around, that it was worth it all. As Tony Campolo declares, "It may be Friday, but Sunday's coming!"

Rewarded for Your Faith

For your reward is great in heaven, for so they persecuted the prophets who were before you.
— *Matthew 5:12b*

This audience of early believers never experienced the rewards American Christian culture has been propagating, presenting and proclaiming in the prosperity message of today: get saved, get rich, get healthy, get popular, get powerful and get successful. Of course, that message is usually followed up with how much seed money you will need to mail in.

Those are *not* the rewards that God has promised to those who place their faith and trust in Him. While He is a "rewarder of those who diligently seek Him," it is imperative that we *define* the reward that God grants to those who demonstrate faith.

The Bible is not silent on this issue; in fact, the entire eleventh chapter of Hebrews is given to demonstrate what faith is, some examples of who had it, how we can get it and what it does. These "people of old"—Abel, Enoch, Noah, Abraham, Sarah, Isaac, Jacob, Joseph, Moses, Joshua and Rahab—never ate what the proponents of the prosperity message dish out, but they were rewarded. Their reward for faith? The approval of God.

That's it. The confidence, assurance and blessing of knowing that you are right with God. That when you take the steps that He has approved, you will be protected, provided for and the recipient of His promises.

Being able to lie down at night and know that whatever tomorrow holds, you know who holds tomorrow. That is a reward that is far better than good health, lots of money, a stable job and a nice house.

I'll take a great God in glory over any good thing on earth any moment of any day. It has worked for 24 years, and I am not about to trade down today!

Rewards Build Faith

Simply put, when God rewards our faith, our faith grows. Because God has demonstrated His ability in our past, we can be confident of His authority in our present and celebrate what we will achieve in the future!

When Abraham stepped out from the comfort and security of his own land to venture out into the unknown, he saw the hand of God move and he was rewarded. So that by the time he was asked to offer his only son, Isaac, he had a past with God and his faith was built up so much in Him that he gladly spoke up, stepped out and surrendered to His will.

Most of us have a past with God. I have a past with God. Let me share a little about what God has done in our family. In 1994, after years of seeing infertility specialists, and suffering through a miscarriage, my wife became pregnant. She was classified as high risk, placed on all kinds of supplements and remained under the watchful eye of our doctor. About three months into the pregnancy my wife was walking down the hallway of our home when she dropped to the floor in pain and declared that something was wrong. I ran the other direction into the living room, hit the floor and cried out to God in prayer. This is the daughter I talked about earlier who is serving in the Air Force.

In 1996 my wife got pregnant again. This time the nine months were rather uneventful, but the labor was drawn out and hard. When our middle daughter was delivered, she was paralyzed on one side of her face due to the use of forceps, as she had breeched. The doctors did not know if this would be permanent or temporary, so we prayed. God healed her, and she is the most beautiful young lady, also presently serving in the United States Air Force.

Because God has demonstrated His ability in our past, we can be confident of His authority in our present and celebrate what we will achieve in the future.

Then, in 1999, we had a surprise when my wife became pregnant again. During a routine ultrasound, at about three months, the expression on the nurse's face concerned us, and when she dismissed herself, mid-test, to go get a doctor, we knew that something was wrong. That day ended in a conference room with our doctor, our nurse and a counselor as they informed us that the ultrasound revealed that our child would be born with spina bifida, and that the collective recommendation was to terminate the pregnancy. Well, by that time in our lives, after all that we had been through with our other children, we just looked at that group of "experts" and basically said, "You all better buckle up because our God is about to show up!" And, show up He did! Our youngest daughter just celebrated her sweet sixteenth birthday and is healthy and beautiful! Again, because God has demonstrated His ability in our past, we can be confident of His authority in our present and celebrate what we will achieve in the future.

Now, I am not saying that God always chooses to fix everything that is broken down here. Remember the list of my current ailments? What I am saying is that we can trust Him based on the history He has with us. Even if you just look to the past, at what He did on the cross, we can move forward with the confidence that He will provide in the future.

I have a past with an Almighty God, so I have no problem believing that God will work everything out in the end and that He will reward me one day as His child!

Final Thoughts

Well this has been quite the journey! We have been poor, mourned, displayed meekness, hungered and thirsted after the things of God, displayed mercy, shunned hypocrisy and brought peace to a chaotic world, with our ultimate reward being persecution—causing us to run around the room, hands in the air, skipping and jumping for joy as if we had won the lottery!

How? Because:

1. Your reward in heaven is great!

James says, "Blessed is the man who remains steadfast under trial, for when he has stood the test he will receive the crown of life, which God has promised to those who love him" (James 1:12). We will receive crowns! And, Revelation gives us a clear picture of what we will be doing with our crowns, or rewards, in heaven: "the twenty-four elders fall down before him who is seated on the throne and worship him who lives forever and ever. They cast their crowns before the throne..." (Revelation 4:10).

I remember as a child being invited to a birthday party by a friend. My friend told me at school that no presents were required, just to come over and watch movies and play games. Well, there I stood that night in his living room as he opened presents from everyone else that came. I felt like a heel, like I didn't even deserve to be his friend or attend his party. I never want to feel that way again. You see, the rewards that Jesus is speaking of are not for our glory but for His! And, we can live our lives in such a way down here that we don't have to feel like a heel one day up there.

2. This world has no claim on your reward!

I can't think of a better story to make this point than that of John Chrysostom. Chrysostom was a godly leader in the fourth-century church, who preached so strongly against sin that he offended the unscrupulous Empress Eudoxia as well as many church officials.

When summoned before Emperor Arcadius, Chrysostom was threatened with banishment if he did not cease his uncompromising preaching.

His response was, "Sire, you cannot banish me, for the world is my Father's house."

"Then I will slay you," Arcadius said.

"Nay, but you cannot, for my life is hid with Christ in God," came the answer.

"Your treasures will be confiscated," was the next threat, to which John replied, "Sire, that cannot be, either. My treasures are in heaven, where none can break through and steal."

"Then I will drive you from man, and you will have no friends left!" was the final, desperate warning.

"That you cannot do, either," answered John, "for I have a Friend in heaven who has said, 'I will never leave you or forsake you.'"

John was indeed banished, first to Armenia and then farther away to Pityus on the Black Sea, to which he never arrived because he died on the way. But neither the banishment nor his death disproved or diminished his claims. The things that he valued most highly not even an emperor could take from him.

And, it is not enough that we are persecuted, for that comes externally and quite often; it is out of our control. What is in our control is the attitude in which that persecution is addressed. Hebrews 10:34 gives us insight as to the proper attitude: "For you had compassion on those in prison, and you **joyfully accepted** the plundering of your property, since you knew that you yourselves had a **better possession** and an abiding one" (Hebrews 10:34).

Joyfully accepted the plundering of their property! What? We freak out when Dish Network drops the Fox channel and when the cost of stamps increases by two cents! Our world is turned upside down when we lose a job, our health or a loved one. These folks joyfully accepted being dragged out of their homes, losing their jobs, being separated from their families and even facing the prospect of a painful death by torture. Joyfully accepted! Not tolerated or put up with, but accepted radical persecution with joy! While the persecution was radical, so was their joyful response. That is how they were able to change the world; they were Being the Believing.

How could they joyfully accept all of the trials that came into their lives? Because they knew they had a better possession. Matthew 13:44 reads, "The kingdom of heaven is like treasure hidden in a field, which a man found and covered up. Then in his *joy* he goes and sells all that he has and buys that field." This man found something valuable, and so he went and sold all that he had and purchased a field that, in the eyes of the world, seemed to be a waste of money. Folks treated him as crazy, but he was able to smile because he knew he had a better possession!

The world may not want to see and understand our better possession in Christ. The cross may be foolishness to them because they refuse to taste and see that the Lord is good. But we have seen and understood what we have in Christ. The cross is not foolishness to us but, rather, the door by which we have access to God, our sure and steadfast anchor of the soul. Since we have tasted and we have found the Lord to be good, we can walk through this life with a smile on our face, accepting any trial, trouble or tribulation with joy in our hearts, a spring in our step and our head held high—because we have a better possession, and an abiding one, in the salvation of our Lord!

If you are Being the Believing, persecution will come; the key is to use that persecution as a stage on which to communicate to this world that Jesus Christ is enough.

CHAPTER TEN

Start Being the Believing

Being the Believing is so much more than walking down the aisle of a church, making an emotional plea, being baptized, or having your name written on the membership roll, or even singing in the choir, teaching a small group class or preaching a sermon. It is all about a transformation in your life from an encounter with the Son of God, Jesus Christ. Being the Believing is the difference between doing good and being good.

I hope you have discovered the joy that comes from giving up on doing good and allowing God to fill you with good. And, I hope that Being the Believing marks your life as you show this world, by your works, that you now have a power within.

I want to share a true story as related by Dr. George Pentecost:

A distinguished Christian lady was recently spending a few weeks at a hotel at Long Branch, and an attempt was made to induce her to attend a dance, in order that the affair might have prestige bestowed by her presence, as she stood high in society. She declined all the importunities of her friends, and finally an honorable senator tried to persuade her to attend, saying, "Miss B., this is quite a harmless affair, and we want to have the exceptional honor of your presence." "Senator," said the lady, "I cannot do it. I am a Christian. I never do anything during my summer vacation, or wherever I go, that will injure the influence I have over the girls of my Sunday School class." The senator bowed, and said, "I honor you; if there were more Christians like you, more men like myself would become Christians."

When hard times come, tears are shed, and hearts are hurting, know this; there is no hurt on earth that heaven cannot heal!

Being the Believing is all about advancing through the beatitudinal ladder. It is a life that enjoys the benefits of being a child of the King, and of being so excited and passionate about those benefits that you can't wait to share this status with others. Being the Believing means that we have:

- **Access to the Throne of God**

There was a time when people trembled at the voice of God and hid from the presence of God. Terrifying was His presence on that Holy Mountain, lit up with lightening and booming with thunder. The average person dared not approach the mountain of God, enter into the Holy of Holies or even walk too close to His furniture, lest they be smote with the wrath of God.

That was all before Jesus came to fulfill the law and take us from a dispensation of Law to the Dispensation of Grace!

Hebrews 12:22 says, "You have come unto mount Sion and unto the city of the living God, the heavenly Jerusalem...." Mountains will fade, tabernacles and temples will crumble and even our precious church buildings will be destroyed because they are all temporal, but our relationship with God is not material or external; rather, it is spiritual and internal. We can walk, talk, fellowship and worship with God anywhere and at any time. This world can't touch the eternal, and circumstance doesn't have to affect the internal. There are so many "Christians" who are NOT living out this belief. They might sing "Power in the Blood" on Sunday and even throw out an "Amen" or two when they hear these truths, but the moment they get some bad news from the doctor, an unexpected phone call or that bill in the mailbox, their worlds are flipped upside down and defeat marks their very lives.

When hard times come, tears are shed, and hearts are hurting, know this; there is no hurt on earth that heaven cannot heal! As children of God we can, according to Hebrews 4:16, "boldly enter into His throne room of grace."

Oh, the joy to know that whatever the time, wherever the place, whoever the seeker, that the living, fearful, terrible, awesome, mighty, powerful God is giving us the invitation to come to His mountain, sit on His furniture and enter into His presence without fear of wrath but to experience His love, mercy and grace. Being the Believing means that as we navigate through this life full of trials, tribulations and troubles, we can have a confidence and assurance that comes from the knowledge that our God has filled us with power and given us a purpose.

And, Being the Believing means that we have a future!

Adoration with the Throng before God:
(Revelation 7:11)

While we have church services down here that are powerful and engaging, glimpses of glory where the power and presence of Christ is felt, they will only be glimpses of glory until we leave this world. But, there is coming a day when we will take those glimpses of glory for an extended journey into forever! What a day that will be, when my Jesus I shall see—when I look upon His face, the One who saved me by His grace. When He takes me by the hand and leads me through the Promised Land, what a day, glorious day, that will be! Being the Believing means that no matter our lot in this life, we will be trading up in the next!

And, Being the Believing means that when life is over and eternity is about to start, we will have:

Acceptance in the Court of God: (Revelation 14:13)

I had a bad experience in 1988 when I was pulled over by a young, cocky and angry State Police officer who was confronted with a young, cocky and angry Tom. He won because he had a gun! He handcuffed me, threw me in the back of his car, drove me to the station and handcuffed me in a cell, and there I waited. I was scared and anxious and did not want to stand before a judge in a court of law, for I was guilty. To this day, whenever I hear a siren or see those blue and red lights flashing, I am that young man in the cell, scared all over again. Oh friend, let me tell you the good news today! One day we will stand before the Judge of All, and because of what Jesus Christ has done, we will not have to plead guilty, not guilty or insanity, but simply plead the name of Jesus! Nothing to the throne I bring; simply to the cross I cling!

Being the Believing is a life that speaks of an understanding that the only One we need to please can be pleased by Being the Believing.

Closing Challenge

In the 1991 movie Hook, Robin Williams plays the grown up Peter Pan, who has returned to Neverland and finds himself trying to prove, to the still young Lost Boys, that he is in fact, Peter Pan. The Lost Boys are unable to recognize Peter as he has grown old, gained weight, is wearing glasses and has wrinkles. Tinker Bell, who knows this aged man to be the real Peter Pan, convinces some of the Lost Boys to give Peter a second look. After everyone has given up, the smallest of the Lost Boys makes his way over to Peter, guides him down to his knees, so that he can look at him face to face, and gives Peter another look over. He removes Peter's glasses, and with both hands pushes back the wrinkles on his forehead, straightens out the wrinkles around his eyes and then pushes the wrinkles on his cheeks far out of the way to remove the many years. While holding the wrinkles back, he looks at Peter in the eyes and declares, "Oh, there you are Peter!" a revelation that causes many of the cynical and unbelieving Lost Boys to rush over with joy and become filled again with hope.

I believe this to be the problem with the Bride of Christ today; we have allowed complacency to fatten the church, selfishness to add many wrinkles, and organization, legalism and politics to dull her vision. Meanwhile, the world around us still hears and sees us but is unable to recognize the once purpose-driven organism that had the power to change the world. I am convinced that once we start Being the Believing, the lost people in this world will give us another look over, push back our wrinkles, dysfunction and sin and declare, "Oh, there you are church!" Imagine what would happen if we all started Being the Believing.

This world is in desperate need of hope and joy, the question remains, will you bring it to them by Being the Believing?

About the Author

Thomas McCracken is the founding pastor of CommUNITY Church in Salem, Virginia, a theologically conservative ministry affiliated with the Southern Baptist Conservatives of Virginia, and serves as Adjunct Faculty at Virginia Western Community College as a Professor of the Liberal Arts and Sciences Division.

Tom is a gifted communicator who has been highlighted on national television for his innovative methods of spreading the gospel. Tom has earned degrees in business and theology and is currently working toward his Ed.D. through Liberty University in Lynchburg, Virginia.

About SermonToBook.Com

SermonToBook.com began with a simple belief: that sermons should be touching lives, *not* collecting dust. That's why we turn sermons into high-quality books that are accessible to people all over the globe.

Turning your sermon or sermon series into a book exposes more people to God's Word, better equips you for counseling, adds credibility to your ministry, and even helps make ends meet during tight times.

John 21:25 tells us that the world itself couldn't contain the books that would be written about the work of Jesus Christ. Our mission is to try anyway. Because, in Heaven, there will no longer be a need for sermons or books. Our time is now.

If God so leads you, we'd love to work with you on your sermon or sermon series.

Visit www.sermontobook.com to learn more.

Notes

1. Bartlett, E. M. "Victory in Jesus."

2. Colson, Charles. *Who Speaks for God?* Tyndale, 1994.

3. Piper, John. "God Is Most Glorified in Us When We Are Most Satisfied in Him." Desiring God, 13 October 2012. http://www.desiringgod.org/sermons/god-is-most-glorified-in-us-when-we-are-most-satisfied-in-him

4. LaVey, Anton Szandor. *The Satanic Bible*. HarperCollins, 1976.

5. Piper, John. "Why I Abominate the Prosperity Gospel." Desiring God, 29 October 2008. http://www.desiringgod.org/interviews/why-i-abominate-the-prosperity-gospel

6. O'Donnell, Douglas Sean. *Matthew: All Authority in Heaven and on Earth*. Preaching the Word. Ed. R. Kent Hughes. Crossway, 2013.

7. MacArthur, John. *Matthew 1–7*. The MacArthur New Testament Commentary. Moody, 1985.

8. ten Boom, Corrie. "I'm Still Learning to Forgive." Guideposts, 1972. From *The Hiding Place*. Chosen Books, 1971.

9. Hughes, R. Kent. *The Sermon on the Mount: The Message of the Kingdom*. ESV ed. Preaching the Word. Crossway, 2013.

10. Peterson, John Willard. "Heaven Came Down." 1961.

11. Osteen, Joel. *Your Best Life Now: 7 Steps to Living at Your Full Potential*. FaithWords, 2004.

12. MacArthur, John. Ibid.

13. Warren, Rick. *The Purpose Driven Life*. Zondervan, 2002.

14. Rogers, Kenny. "The Gambler." 1978.

15. "Reba the Landlord." *Reba*. Season 5, Ep. 17. 17 March 2006.